Action Research in Catholic Schools:

A Step-by-Step Guide for Practitioners

SECOND EDITION

Action Research in Catholic Schools Series

CATHOLIC EDUCATION STUDIES DIVISION

Alliance for Catholic Education Press
at the University of Notre Dame

Action Research in Catholic Schools:

A Step-by-Step Guide for Practitioners

SECOND EDITION

Anthony C. Holter
James M. Frabutt

ALLIANCE FOR CATHOLIC EDUCATION PRESS
at the University of Notre Dame

Notre Dame, Indiana

Copyright © 2011

Alliance for Catholic Education Press
University of Notre Dame
107 Carole Sandner Hall
Notre Dame, IN 46556
http://acepress.nd.edu

ISBN 978-1-935788-07-2

Text design by Julie Wernick Dallavis
Cover design by Mary Jo Adams Kocovski

Library of Congress Cataloging-in-Publication Data

Holter, Anthony C., 1977-
  Action research in Catholic schools : step-by-step guide for practitioners / Anthony
C. Holter, James M. Frabutt. -- 2nd ed.
       p. cm. -- (Action research in Catholic schools series)
  Includes bibliographical references.
  Summary: "Textbook for conducting and preparing an action research study and
report in the Catholic school context"--Provided by publisher.
  ISBN 978-1-935788-07-2 (pbk. : alk. paper) 1. Catholic Church--Education--Unit-
ed States. 2. Catholic schools--Research--United States. 3. Action research--United
States. I. Frabutt, James M., 1972- II. Title.
  LC501.H57 2011
  371.071'273--dc23
                                    2011028293

Contents

1

Action Research in Catholic Schools: An Introduction

Our Catholic schools "proceed *ex corde Ecclesiae*, from the very heart of the Church," to provide exceptional academic preparation and spiritual formation for millions of Catholic school children annually (Miller, 2006, p. vii). As such, the Catholic school is the nexus, the meeting place, of the sacred and the secular. Teachers and leaders in Catholic schools are charged with the interlocking educational tasks of forming the intellect and the soul of those children entrusted to their care. And there is recognizable difficulty in doing this. As a teacher in or principal of a Catholic school, you know how challenging it can be to ensure that through the "knowledge students gradually acquire of the world, life and man is illumined by faith" (Vatican Council II, 1965, para. 20).

So how will you respond to the challenges that face you as educators and leaders in Catholic schools? How do you ensure that you are developing policies and enacting pedagogies that create positive educational opportunities for your students? Action research is an innovative educational research methodology that provides a general framework and set of specific, research-based tools designed to assess and respond to pressing needs in our Catholic schools. Action research does not provide one answer for all educational issues; it is not a panacea. In fact, by its very design, action research is meant to be adaptive and responsive to the specific needs, challenges, and issues facing each Catholic school community.

As a practitioner in a Catholic school, you are perfectly positioned to apply the tools of action research to the needs in your school community. We are fully aware that engaging in applied educational research may seem daunting at first, but our experience has been that action research is a fulfilling and vital component to effective school leadership (James, Milenkiewicz, & Bucknam, 2008; Wamba, 2006). This book was designed specifically for you—teachers and leaders in Catholic schools—as an entrée into action research and a step-by-step guide for the technical aspects of designing, implementing, evaluating, and publishing your action research project. Admittedly, it is beyond the scope and purpose of this text to examine the broad epistemological and theological components of action research; for that level of theoretical analysis, see *Research, Action, and Change: Leaders Reshaping Catholic Schools* (Frabutt, Holter, & Nuzzi, 2008). It is sufficient to say that action research is not some special form of Catholic research. However, the ways in which practitioners apply the methods of action research to real world educational issues affirms the dignity of persons and importance of community, advances our commitment to social justice, and animates our Catholic faith. Throughout this text, we will highlight specific areas within the process of action research that are particularly suited for just such an integration of research methods and tenets of our Catholic faith.

Each chapter in this text addresses a specific component or module within the overall framework of action research that, if followed to completion, will lead to a well-designed action research project (AR project) and comprehensive action research report (AR report). Far from a static record of research methods and findings, this text is meant to inspire innovative action research projects that advance "courageous renewal on the part of the Catholic school" (Congregation for Catholic Education, 1998, para. 3).

Action Research: The Tripartite Definition

One way to think about action research is along a continuum ranging from an immediate, point-in-time response to classroom issues (e.g., differentiating instruction to respond to student difficulty with a specific math concept) to a more developed, systematic response over an extended period of time (e.g., developing a training program for lay teachers to promote ownership of the unique charism of the school's founding religious order). This breadth in the continuum of action research has produced equally broad-ranging definitions. Some practitioners and researchers define action research as "any systematic inquiry conducted by teachers, administrators, counselors, or others with a vested interest in the teaching and learning process or environment for the purpose of gathering information" (Mertler, 2009, p. 4), while others view action research as "a methodology integrating social science inquiry with participants' practical action so that all concerned have a sense of agency rather than constructing themselves as powerless" (Somekh, 2006, p. 1).

For the purposes of this book, and the modules delineated in the following chapters, we have synthesized and distilled these many definitions and expressions of action research into three major components. Action research is: (a) systematic inquiry, (b) oriented toward positive change in the school or classroom, and (c) embraces a participatory approach that is practitioner-driven. For a detailed overview of the history and conceptualization of action research, see Frabutt et al. (2008, pp. 5-24).

The definition and orienting framework utilized in this text is admittedly aligned with the highly structured, developed, and systematic end of the action research continuum. In fact, the framework, modules, and examples contained herein were developed to facilitate the successful completion of a capstone research project by candidates for the Master of Arts in Educational Administration degree in the Mary Ann Remick Leadership Program at the University of Notre Dame. This is certainly not the only way to conduct action research, but we have found it to be one method that is accessible and effective for teachers and leaders in Catholic schools.

Before we proceed with the mechanics of action research, let us consider each element of the tripartite operational definition.

Action Research Is Systematic Inquiry

Sound methodology is essential for all forms of educational research. In our conceptual framework, traditional methods of educational research are employed to develop, implement, and evaluate action research projects. These traditional research methods provide the specific design, processes, and tools that make action research both rigorous and systematic. What this means practically is that action researchers will use appropriate design, procedure, and analytic tools in the implementation and assessment of their AR project. Additionally, the final AR report will follow style and content guidelines of a traditional research paper. There is evidence to suggest that when teachers and leaders engage in practitioner-driven, systematic inquiry they "acquire habits and skills of inquiry that they use beyond the research experience" (Zeichner, 2001, p. 279). It is our sincere hope that the analytic skills honed through action research will transcend any single project and become incorporated in the myriad skills, dispositions, and resources you employ as a Catholic school leader.

Action Research Is Change-Oriented

Ultimately, we engage in action research to bring about change in policies and practices that positively affects students in our classrooms, schools, and communities. Action research is not meant to remain bound or static, but to be applied and transformative. We have strong and mounting evidence that action research can indeed facilitate lasting positive changes in Catholic schools. Former students and current Catholic school leaders across the country adopted this transformative stance toward teaching and leading through action research when they created a mentoring program to address the social and academic needs of conditionally admitted, at-risk, high school students (Kmack, 2008), developed a specialized reading program for English language learners in a parish elementary school (Asmar, 2008a, 2008b), or evaluated the academic and interpersonal effects of a new program that provides a laptop computer to middle school students (Bayer, 2008). These examples provide a glimpse of action researchers as change agents with the potential "to enliven and enrich Catholic schools through systematic, relevant, and change-oriented action research" (Frabutt et al., 2008, p. 21).

Action Research Is Collaborative and Practitioner-Driven

To say that action research is practitioner-driven affirms the important voice, experience, and expertise of the teacher or principal as educational leader and advocate in the school. The practitioner-driven approach to action research challenges the traditional top-down model of scholarship where knowledge originates in the academy from scholar experts, and filters down through the literature to practitioners at the school level (Gaventa & Cornwall, 2001). On the contrary, action researchers seek to integrate the role of researcher and practitioner, and to facilitate collaborative relationships with colleagues in the school and broader community. When action research is conducted in this way, it effectively bridges the gap between scholar and practitioner, between research and practice, and often produces innovative and effective solutions to specific issues within the school community (Mertler, 2009; Zeichner, 2001).

The successful action research project is dependent upon each of these three components working in harmony: systematic inquiry that is practitioner-driven and change-oriented. If any one of these components is absent from the research design, the process and product really are not action research.

AR Insight

❝ The journey through action research was challenging, demanding, and time-consuming; however, the benefits to my school community have been empowering and uplifting. **❞**

About This Book

This text is a step-by-step guide to action research in Catholic schools—a jumping off point for practitioner-driven inquiry oriented to positive change and school renewal. Some of you may be new to the process of educational research; others may have experience with formal or informal research in your school or your classroom. No matter your level of experience or comfort with educational research, this text is designed to provide both an introduction to action research and a series of modules, examples, and practice exercises that guide you through each step of the action research process and build toward an independent AR project and final AR report.

We recommend first reading the text in its entirety to gain a sense of how each component, each module, contributes to the conceptual and methodological framework of action research that we espouse. Once you have read the entire text, we recommend using it as a workbook by completing the included mini-lab exercises step-by-step as you proceed through your own AR project. This incremental movement through each module will facilitate the development of a compelling research topic and comprehensive AR report.

Remember, research is not the answer but a way to discover effective and meaningful responses to the important educational issues facing our students and our Catholic schools. As such, action research is a process of discovery that is not exhausted with one research question nor is it finished in one project or intervention. Action research requires your sustained commitment as practitioner-researcher "to ensure that Catholic schools have administrators and teachers who are prepared to provide an exceptional educational experience for young people—one that is both truly Catholic and of the highest academic quality" (United States Conference of Catholic Bishops, 2005, para. 1).

FEATURES OF THE TEXT	
Mini-Labs	Mini-Labs are embedded throughout the text to help you conceptualize, design, and revise important components of your own AR project. You may complete each mini-lab in this workbook or in your own research journal.
AR Insights	AR Insights are tips and suggestions for the successful completion of your own AR project. Many of these insights come directly from graduates of the program—individuals who have successfully completed an AR project just like the one you are developing right now!
Action Research in Action	At the end of each chapter we include samples of an AR project in progress. This example paper is based on a hypothetical research scenario regarding Saint Michael Parish and School. A full version of this AR report is included at the end of this text.
Sample AR Report	The Sample AR Report is included at the end of this text as a guide and example for the construction of your own final AR report. Specific formatting requirements for the American Psychological Association (APA) and sample writing elements are included for each of the major sections of a research report.

IMPORTANT NOTE

The Action Research in Action and Sample AR Report components of this text are NOT authentic research. They are designed to be examples of the process and final product of an AR project. Both elements are based on a hypothetical research scenario and the data are entirely fabricated. Furthermore, portions of the paper are intentionally left incomplete as indicated by the notation **[section continues]**. In your own AR report you would, of course, continue on with the writing or analysis. As such, no part of this AR paper should be cited as an original or authentic research report.

2

Choosing Action Research

As outlined in chapter 1, the tripartite nature of action research demands systematic research, an orientation toward change, and a participatory approach that is practitioner-driven. Beyond those characteristics, which many list as the defining elements of action research, we believe that action research holds special promise for Catholic educators. That is, conceived within the context of Catholic education, action research is undergirded by the twin values of spirituality and community (Frabutt, Holter, & Nuzzi, 2008). As educators continually discern their vocation, a spirituality enlivened by positive social change is allowed to flourish through action research. Coupled with a singular call to Christian community—so elemental to the nature of Catholic schools—we believe that "no less than full scale renewal and reinvigoration of Catholic schools is possible when educational leaders evince an inquiry-oriented approach to their ministry in the classrooms, schools, and parishes that they hold dear" (Frabutt et al., 2008, p. 1).

Knowing When the Stage Is Set for Action Research

There are a few common indicators when a situation is ripe for action research. First, consider whether you have ever been in a faculty meeting, a unit meeting, or a planning discussion with a colleague, and the answer to a probing question that you posed is, "Well, that's what we've always done." Teachers and administrators in Catholic schools will readily confirm that often what passes for "best practice" in their building is not necessarily what is empirically supported, evidence-based, or founded on current educational research. Rather, "best practice" is little more than "the way we do it around here." Curricula, disciplinary practices, assessment techniques, even the way the school Christmas show unfolds can be locked in an organizational inertia that appears beyond reproach—or at least serious questioning.

Another indication that action research is needed occurs when popular opinion and the prevailing common wisdom insist that some practice—a novel teaching tactic, an alternative grading approach, a social skills intervention—works. Typically, any serious challenge of the unexamined practice in question is met with *"Everybody* knows that *x* works." Too often in schools we may do what is safe, what appears tried and true, and what many have long accepted without deep questioning. Action research is an approach uniquely suited to ask questions about effectiveness, efficacy, and program/practice improvement. Even in cases where the practice in question turns out to be largely successful, action research identifies strategies for refinement and growth.

In line with the social justice orientation of action research, a third indication that a context is conducive to action research is when you feel compelled to be more responsive and/or engaged with a growing need. For example, a school that has recently undergone dramatic shifts in the racial/ethnic composition of its enrolled families may need to reconsider how it addresses the needs of English language learners. Such a scenario unfolded as Immaculate Conception Catholic School in Laurel, Mississippi, made strides to accommodate and meet the academic literacy needs of Hispanic students (Asmar, 2008a, 2008b). When change is clearly necessary, action research allows educators to make the case for change through a systematic, data-based presentation of locally relevant needs. Careful documentation of needs and a careful exploration of potentially effective responses pave the way for stakeholders to marshal the resources, support, and momentum that they need in order to facilitate real change.

Perhaps you already have an idea about something in your school community that you would like to explore more fully or examine more closely. If this is the case, then you have already begun to develop a research topic.

Choosing a Research Topic

A research topic is the "broad subject matter that a researcher wishes to address in a study" (Creswell, 2008, p. 74). Some see this initial step in research—identifying a research topic—as one of the most challenging. On the other hand, this initial effort is where creativity and opportunity merge. Consider this step as an open and engaging part of the process—because you can follow your own interests and take some time to wonder. Indeed, some authors call this stage "finding your wondering," which materializes "as professional passions at the nexus of a teacher's work, his or her teaching dilemmas or 'felt difficulties'" (Dana & Yendol-Silva, 2003, p. 14). We offer here some considerations, strategies, and tips to start your project with confidence and vision.

A first consideration in selecting a topic is to follow your own personal interests (see Mini-Lab 2.1). In fact, several authors have stressed the importance of autobiographical reflection. Your own lived experience is the greatest source of potential research questions. Drawing upon your own personal beliefs, history, values, and experiences is a natural starting point for research (Hendricks, 2006; Rearick & Feldman, 1999). Keep in mind that since you will devote significant time and effort to this research effort, the topic should be something in which you are personally and professionally vested. As Sagor (2005) noted,

> If a teacher's action research addresses an issue that is of significant personal or professional importance, then invariably, the time spent conducting the research is well spent. However, if the issue under consideration turns out to be peripheral to the concerns of the researcher, then even the smallest investment of energy is resented. (p. 11)

Mini-Lab 2.1: Formulating a Research Topic

As you begin to formulate your research topic, consider the following questions:

- What are the topics that most energize you as a professional educator?
- What aspects of your school and parish life are most interesting?
- Have you encountered—through current educational research journals or current Catholic educational research (e.g., *Catholic Education: A Journal of Inquiry and Practice*)—topics that you find provocative or engaging?

AR Insight

We have found that the more central or connected your topic is to your professional responsibilities in the school and your personal interests, the more likely it is that you will devote sufficient time and energy to your research. Consider this quote from a current Catholic school action researcher:

❝ Choosing the right topic was the most important decision I made in this process. I had to think about the real needs of our school community, determine the existence of research on the topic, and the most significant factor was that I had to be passionate about the issue. I needed to select a project that would be worth researching for hours upon hours in the library, searching for articles, reading through journals, and synthesizing the information. **❞**

A second consideration for selecting an action research topic is that the area of inquiry should be responsive to parish, school, or community needs. The best action research projects will bear on the school community in a manner that is timely, useful, and relevant. You might reflect on questions like those listed in Mini-Lab 2.2.

Mini-Lab 2.2: Parish, School, or Community Needs

- What are some of the perceived areas of need at your school?
- What programs, policies, and procedures have been implemented to meet those needs? Are they effective?
- What challenges does your school or parish currently face?
- What educational issues have most concerned faculty, administrators, parents, or students over the past year?

Ultimately, "a good action research question is one that leads to greater understanding of something that you very much need or want to learn more about" (Sagor, 2005, p. 75). In addition to the self-reflective stance outlined earlier, collaborative reflection is another useful strategy to explore potential topics. Talking with your peers or other educational professionals directly helps to form and shape a research topic. If you are a teacher, a discussion with administrators in your building can surface school-specific ideas. If you are a school administrator, consultation with your faculty, school parents, the superintendent, or central office staff would be a useful step. In general, offering your thoughts up to others, seeking feedback, asking questions, and assuming an inquisitive posture sharpens your research topic.

When discerning a topic area, a third consideration is the contextual level at which your project will unfold. A project can be focused at the classroom level, such as when an individual teacher seeks to critically reflect on his or her own evolving curriculum in order to improve both the content and delivery of the course objectives. For example, through pre- and posttesting, focus groups, and interviews, Alokolaro (2008) studied the roll-out of a newly designed course that combined language arts and students' critical use of information resources. Often labeled teacher research, teacher inquiry, or practitioner research, there is an extensive and well-documented lineage (e.g., Anderson, Herr, & Nihlen, 1994; Cochran-Smith & Lytle, 1999; Mohr et al., 2004) of teachers engaging in this type of self-directed, critical analysis of their teaching practice (Richards, 2007), classroom assessment strategies (Hui, 2008), and professional collaboration (Hobson, 2001). When educators do engage in such research, they glean myriad benefits, including a deepened sense of empowerment, heightened engagement, ongoing professional development, and a firmer grasp on their own agency in effecting educational renewal (Hui & Grossman, 2008).

Action research can also be conceived and conducted in a manner that focuses on school-level issues. In this case, multiple classrooms, the entire faculty, or a building-level change in curriculum could be the unit of analysis. One example comes from St.

Paul's Catholic School in Jacksonville Beach, Florida, where the process and academic effect of a shift from traditional to block scheduling has been analyzed through action research (Thompson, 2009). In the Diocese of Oakland, Pierre-Antoine (2008) sought to develop and nurture the unique charism of the Mission San Jose Sisters at St. Edward School through an action research project that involved former principals, current faculty, and newly hired staff. In each case, an individual undertook a project that involved multiple school stakeholders and sought to understand and change processes unfolding at the school level.

Some action research projects pose questions that extend the lens of inquiry beyond the parameters of the school itself. Projects that seek to explore an issue on a diocesan level—at multiple school sites or through surveying all principals, for example—are geared toward understanding a phenomenon through a broader framework. One instance is Frazier's (2008) diocesan survey of administrators to surface their knowledge regarding federal requirements of the Individuals with Disabilities Education Act (IDEA). Because of its scope, knowledge and insight gained from such an inquiry carry the potential to inform diocesan policy and practice.

Another class of projects unfolds at the interface of the school with other entities, such as its neighborhood context, its relationship to other schools, or its outreach into the community. The nature of the school-parish connection also exemplifies this level of analysis. Indeed, McCann-Ojeda (2008) and Burleigh (2009) examined the relationship between the elementary school and the parish, considering the views of parishioners, non-parishioners, school-enrolled, and non-enrolled families.

The range of possible topics for inquiry is boundless, often limited only by one's imagination, creativity, and context. While you will likely have no shortage of topic ideas, Table 2.1 indicates several broad thematic areas within the realm of education that could give rise to a research topic. Reviewing over 100 teacher action research inquiries, the first column identifies what Dana and Yendol-Silva (2003) have termed the eight major passions that have given rise to the bulk of practitioner research. Likewise, the second column of Table 2.1 lists broad potential topic areas (Mertler, 2009).

Table 2.1
Potential Topic Areas

Teacher/educator passions	Sample topic areas
Helping an individual child Improving or enriching curriculum Developing content knowledge Improving teaching strategies and techniques Exploring classroom practices Nexus of personal and professional identities Advocating social justice Understanding teaching and learning context	Classroom environment Instructional materials Classroom management Instructional methods Human development and education Grading and evaluation Conferencing

Now that you have reviewed some general topic areas, articulate your own research topic in Mini-Lab 2.3.

Mini-Lab 2.3: Writing Your Research Topic

As you can see in Table 2.1, research topics are quite broad and are written in phrases. Refining these research topics will come later. For now, consider two broad research topics that are of interest to you.

All initial topic selections, however, are not created equal for pursuing an action research approach. Both internal and external factors can delimit the scope of a feasible undertaking. You may identify an area that interests you greatly and is especially relevant to your school setting, but some pragmatic and logistic considerations are critical to determining the feasibility of the project. These additional considerations are time, resources, and access, which you will explore in Mini-Lab 2.4:

- **Time:** While it is possible to conduct a multi-year action research project, given the rhythms of the academic calendar, many educators wish to complete a cycle of action research in less than a year. It is helpful to think in terms of quarters, semesters, and other important milestones throughout the academic year in conceptualizing a project. Will you be able to complete the project in one year? For example, consider a teacher who wants to assess the impact of her school's new classroom management system, but all classrooms will not have the system in place until after the second quarter. That schedule would not likely allow adequate time to implement the program, collect and analyze data, and make changes to the program before the end of the school year. Will you be able to complete your project given the time constraints of your school calendar?

- **Resources/costs:** Much traditional research that occurs in the private sector and in academia is heavily supported by funding to underwrite the costs of research personnel, travel, equipment, and other items essential to the project. Action researchers are much more entrepreneurial in their approach and may be working individually or in a group, but without the support of formal funding. For these reasons, it is important to consider the amount and kind of materials, resources, travel, and equipment that your topic would require. Are additional support and resources available if needed?

- **Access:** Some topics require a negotiation of access to academic files, computer records, databases, and the like in order to proceed. For example, you may want to assess the impact of a change in block scheduling on academic performance that requires access to diocesan-wide test scores. Is it feasible to negotiate such access? Do you have access to the information sources or data that your research topic requires?

Finally, it is essential to confirm that which started the topic discernment in the first place: Have you actually arrived at an action research topic? There are certain elements that help determine whether your topic has an action research orientation. Sagor (2005) offered three questions to determine whether your inquiry qualifies as action research: (a) Is the focus of your inquiry on your professional action? (b) Are you empowered to adjust future action based on the results? (c) Is improvement possible?

Mini-Lab 2.4: Evaluating Your Research Topic

There are many external factors that impact the feasibility of your research topic. Consider the following questions and revise your research topic accordingly.

1. Time: Will you be able to complete your project given the time constraints of your school calendar?
2. Resources: Are additional support and resources available for the materials, travel, or other items your research topic requires?
3. Access: Do you have access to the sources or data that your research topic requires?

Affirmative responses to each of Sagor's questions ensure that your focus is in your area of professional purview, and that your project may result in an action plan for classroom, school, or parish improvement.

AR Insight

❝ I had a topic that I was very interested in learning more about, which gave me the motivation to put time aside to work on the project. ❞

Stating the Topic as a Research Problem

As mentioned earlier, a statement of topic is a broad articulation of your research interest area. It exists at a level of abstraction that is purposefully general and not linked to a highly particular context. Examples include faculty cohesion and professional learning communities; service learning in Catholic high schools; curricular alignment to support math achievement; and ability grouping for reading literacy. To make the topic researchable, however, requires a process of narrowing the general research topic into a refined set of specific research questions (see Figure 2.1). Just as a

Figure 2.1   Developing Your Research Topic

General	Research Topic	Broad subject matter that a researcher wishes to address in a study; usually stated as a sentence fragment *Example*: Catholic school access and consolidation
	Research Problem	General educational issue, concern, or controversy that the action researcher investigates *Example*: Current trends in Catholic education indicate that Catholic primary and secondary school tuition is increasing, and access to affordable Catholic education in many urban, impoverished areas is decreasing (NCEA, 2008). These conditions negatively affect the accessibility and affordability of Catholic schools for many families in urban communities. As principal of Saint Michael School, it is my job to ensure that Catholic students in this parish have access to a rigorous academic and exceptionally Catholic education.
	Purpose Statement	Statement that advances the overall direction or focus of the research topic *Example*: The purpose of this study is to examine stakeholder perspectives on the accessibility and proposed consolidation of Saint Michael Catholic School.
	Research Question	Fundamental question(s) inherent in the purpose statement *Example*: What is the 5-year enrollment trend at Saint Michael School? What reasons do parents provide for enrolling their children in Saint Michael School? What do stakeholders at Saint Michael School and Parish identify as primary concerns or issues regarding the impact of school consolidation on their school and parish community?
Specific	Specific Item or Question	Specific question or item in a survey, interview, or focus group that addresses some aspect of your research question *Example*: From the list below, rank the top three reasons you enroll your child in Saint Michael School (survey). Tell me about the greatest strength of a Saint Michael education (interview). What are the major benefits and drawbacks of consolidating Saint Michael School with other local Catholic grade schools (focus group)?

funnel is widest at its top and gradually tapers to a limited opening, so too must you proceed from the abstract to the specific—in this case, from a topic to a purpose statement, and on to research questions. Figure 2.1 demonstrates, through the use of the example of Catholic school access, the linkage between topic, purpose, questions, and items. For your next step, complete Mini-Lab 2.5 to transition from a topic statement to a research problem.

Mini-Lab 2.5: Writing a Research Problem

Now that you have chosen an interesting research topic you will write a general research problem describing the importance of your topic in 3-4 sentences. Your research problem should address the following questions:

1. Why have you chosen this topic?
2. Why is your topic a concern or issue?
3. Why is it an important topic to investigate?
4. What is its relevance for your professional practice, school community, and/or personal interest?

The Purpose Statement

The purpose statement is a concise sentence through which the action researcher asserts the primary focus of the proposed project. The purpose statement should flow from the research topic and research problem, providing additional clarity to the proposed research project. The purpose statement can take many forms; most commonly researchers begin with "The purpose of this research was to..." The purpose statement serves an important function in the research paper as a conduit between the general introduction and specific research questions. Complete Mini-Lab 2.6 to develop your purpose statement.

Mini-Lab 2.6: Writing a Purpose Statement

Can you articulate the primary focus of your research project in one sentence? This may be challenging, but will provide a clear and concise motivation for pursuing your particular line of research. Consider the following prompt:

The purpose of this action research was to...

Developing Research Questions

Having outlined the need, importance, justification, and purpose of the research problem above, what questions do you most want to answer? To frame your questions, think about the kinds of answers that would be most helpful to you as a teacher or principal. Sometimes multiple questions are necessary in order to fully explore a topic. In other cases, there may be one major question, followed up with several sub-questions. This step is highly interrelated with the subsequent steps of the project in that thoughtfully crafted research questions guide the content and formatting considerations of most data collection efforts. Furthermore, careful alignment of research questions and specific items used during your data collection will provide clarity in the methods you choose to collect and analyze your data. Turn to Mini-Lab 2.7 to articulate and refine your research questions.

Mini-Lab 2.7: Articulating Research Questions

Write at least two major research questions that align with the research topic, research problem, and purpose statement you developed in Mini-Lab 2.5 and 2.6. Refer to Figure 2.1 for ideas on wording and construction.

Thinking Ahead to Method

Now that you have articulated some specific research questions, consider what kinds of data are likely to yield the information required to answer those questions. How will you measure key variables of interest? Who will you need to contact and/or interview to access this information? Will you have access to the necessary data and people? Are any of these data highly sensitive or otherwise difficult to access? Will they be available in time to be used for your research project? Complete Mini-Lab 2.8 to identify your sources.

Mini-Lab 2.8: Identifying Your Sources

List at least three sources that will likely provide important data for your research. These sources may include materials (e.g., test scores) and stakeholders (e.g., parents of your students).

Assuring an Ethical Approach to Action Research

University Approval

When teachers and administrators conduct research as part of the degree requirements of their academic program, universities exert some oversight regarding ethical research practices in students' research projects. At the University of Notre Dame, such oversight is provided by the Human Subjects Institutional Review Board (HSIRB). Before any university-affiliated research with human participants can begin, the

HSIRB requires submission of a research proposal that describes the major elements of a study. The guidelines ask for information regarding the background and purpose of the study, a discussion of study procedures, and consideration of study risks and benefits, with special attention to procedures to obtain participants' consent.

The primary objective of this board and others like it is to ensure that several key ethical principles are upheld in the conduct of research, namely respect for persons, beneficence, and justice. Based on both international consensus (World Medical Association, 1964) and the Code of Federal Regulations, one can find a full description of these principles in the Belmont Report (National Commission, 1979). The first ethical principle is that of respect for persons, which highlights the autonomy and agency of research participants and ensures their right to choose to give or deny consent to participate. It also mandates that those with diminished autonomy are entitled to protection. The second principle—beneficence—is best understood as the imperative to do no harm; it holds that in making ethical research decisions, one must maximize benefits and minimize potential harm or risk to participants. Justice is the third major ethical principle and it poses the question, who ought to bear the benefits of research and bear its burdens?

In educational action research there are particular issues to which practitioner researchers should be attentive. First, practitioner researchers should be aware of potential dual role conflicts. These conflicts can occur when the role of researcher and practitioner overlap. For example, a dual role conflict is possible when a principal studies differentiated classroom instruction practices among the faculty. As the principal conducts observations and evaluates classroom pedagogy, it may be unclear to faculty if the data will be used for purposes of the research project or for an official performance review. Since the principal is responsible for both data collection and annual reviews, a potential conflict arises: What "hat" is the principal wearing, and when? Therefore, the practitioner researcher must make every effort to clearly articulate the purpose of action research and delineate the uses of data gleaned from the project. Enacting these precautions will not eliminate dual role conflicts, but they will minimize the potential risks to participants and threats to the validity of the data.

Another important issue for practitioner researchers to be attentive to is informed consent among students. According to the Department of Health and Human Services, students under the age of 18 are considered children, a vulnerable population, and therefore are subject to special precautions under most HSIRB guidelines (see Federal Register, 45 CFR Part 46, Additional Protection for Children Involved as Subjects in Research). In addition to normal precautions to prevent harm or risk to participants, children require both the consent of their parent or guardian and individual assent. That is to say both the child and his or her parent/guardian can choose or refuse to participate at any time without penalty or prejudice. Sample consent and assent forms can be found in Appendix C in the Sample AR Report in chapter 9.

One exception to the requirements of consent and assent is if the research being conducted falls under "normal educational practices" (45 CFR 46). Normal educational practices include research conducted in "commonly accepted educational settings" and on "normal educational practices" (45 CFR 46). If you are conducting research in your school or classroom it is likely that you meet the criteria for the exemption stated above, but only a university institutional review board or appropriate diocesan committee/office can grant such exemption.

The two examples provided here are common to most educational action research, but are not exhaustive of all the circumstances or issues you will encounter when conducting research with human subjects. Before proceeding with your research project make sure that you have received the appropriate university approval, and, at minimum, abide by your commitment to respect for persons, beneficence, and justice (Hammack, 1997; Nolen & Vander Putten, 2007; Pritchard, 2002).

Diocesan Approval

Some dioceses have policies in place that require formal review of a research proposal by an appointed board. For example, the Archdiocese of Washington, DC, requires a research proposal review that considers elements such as the purpose of the study, the population of focus, procedures, timeline, and a full discussion of risks, benefits, informed consent, and provisions for ensuring anonymity/confidentiality (Policy 1360, Archdiocese of Washington; J. McDonald, personal communication, November 6, 2008). This level of review may be more typical in a case where the proposed research is diocesan-wide, affects many schools, or will deliver diocesan-level recommendations. Other dioceses may prefer that research be approved by the superintendent, and others may have no requirements whatsoever for central office review of a research proposal. For teachers conducting research in their own classroom or within their own school, by and large, securing the approval of the principal is the major requirement before proceeding with the research.

Action Research in Action:
Hypothetical Research Scenario

The following hypothetical research scenario is based on actual historical events and contemporary issues facing many urban, Catholic parishes and schools. It will serve as the general case study of this text and specific research topic for the sample AR report at the end of each chapter.

Saint Michael Parish is located in the urban center of a large, Midwestern city. Founded in 1879 by Benedictine Monks, Saint Michael was the spiritual and cultural center of the largely German, immigrant neighborhood. Benedictine Sisters arrived 7 years after the parish was established to open and run Saint Michael School. Saint Michael School served the children of the German immigrants who built the parish and was an extension of the German, Catholic community in that area. For example, many of the Sisters would teach portions of their classes in German. Additionally, the annual school and parish festival was a showcase of classic German food, song, and dance. At its zenith, Saint Michael School taught over 800 students from the neighborhood each year.

Saint Michael Parish still serves a predominantly immigrant population, but much has changed over the past 130 years. Descendants of the original German immigrants have, for the most part, left the neighborhood. In the wake of their departure, the neighborhood has embraced a new cultural identity; it is now a vibrant community enlivened with Hispanic heritage and traditions. In fact, the pastor recently added a second Spanish language Mass to the weekend liturgy schedule. The parish enjoys high weekly Mass attendance, many well-supported outreach ministry efforts, and a cadre of young families who volunteer in many of the parish activities.

Much is new at Saint Michael School, too. The Benedictine Sisters are no longer present, and in 2003 the pastor appointed a lay board of limited jurisdiction to help oversee the school. While parish Mass attendance is on the rise, school enrollment has leveled off over the past 3 years at approximately 175 students in kindergarten through eighth grade. The many parents involved in parish life—through outreach activities, liturgy, and other initiatives—are noticeably absent from school functions and programs.

The level of education these students receive at Saint Michael is comparable to other urban schools in the area, yet 85% of Saint Michael graduates continue their education in a local Catholic high school, graduate, and go on to college. Many outreach programs have been suggested to increase school visibility and enrollment. However, several parishioners and board members are concerned that these outreach initiatives characterize the school as little more than a safe, inexpensive alternative to the public school system.

Saint Michael School provides an excellent education for its students, but has struggled in recent years to meet the financial burdens of an aging building with declining enrollment. At a recent school board meeting the school principal and school board president presented a preliminary plan to consolidate Saint Michael School with three other urban, Catholic schools. This preliminary plan calls for the consolidated school to be located in a new, centrally located building approximately 3 miles from Saint Michael School and Parish.

A sub-committee was formed to examine stakeholder perspectives on the accessibility and proposed consolidation of Saint Michael Catholic School. The committee plans to engage key stakeholder groups likely to speak to these core issues and offer innovative ideas for an action plan to address them. The principal of the school will chair the committee and present a final report to the school board by the end of the academic year.

Action Research in Action:
Overview

Each chapter will conclude with sample exercises or examples to highlight the development of a sample AR report up to that point. These examples are based on the hypothetical Saint Michael School scenario and will respond directly to the focus and content of each individual chapter. The examples are admittedly not exhaustive of all possibilities, but are designed to highlight the salient process and product features of action research. As you read through these sample exercises, consider the parallels with your own action research project.

Research Topic: Catholic School Consolidation

Research Problem:
    Current trends in Catholic education indicate that Catholic primary and secondary school tuition is increasing, and access to affordable Catholic education in many urban, impoverished areas is decreasing (National Catholic Educational Association, 2008). These conditions negatively affect the accessibility of Catholic schools for many families in urban communities. As principal of Saint Michael School, it is my job to ensure that Catholic students in this parish have access to a rigorous academic and exceptionally Catholic education.

Purpose Statement:
    The purpose of this study is to examine stakeholder perspectives on the accessibility and proposed consolidation of Saint Michael Catholic School.

Research Question:
    1. What do stakeholders at Saint Michael School and Parish identify as primary concerns or issues regarding the impact of school consolidation on their school and parish community?
        a. What is the 5-year enrollment trend at Saint Michael School?

Identifying Resources:
    Materials: School enrollment data (approximately 5 years), Parishioner directory/database
    Stakeholders: Pastor of Saint Michael Parish, Parishioners with school-age children who enroll/do not enroll their children at Saint Michael School, Community members

3

Introduction and Literature Review

It is our hope that you have decided on a topic area that you are not only passionate about but one that has immediate relevance and applicability to your school. The next step in continuing your action research project is to formally describe the context that has given rise to your work. You will do so via the opening section of your action research paper, the introduction. Then, having situated your research within its local context, you will relate your topic area to other existing knowledge and discourse on the topic. That process results in the second section of your paper, the literature review. The *Publication Manual of the American Psychological Association* (APA; 2010) does not distinguish between the introduction and literature review. We find that articulating two separate but related sections at the beginning of the research paper provides additional clarity for your chosen research topic. Therefore, this chapter describes the components and purposes of each of those sections in more detail and provides a scaffolded structure for you to follow in developing your own introduction and literature review.

The Introduction

The introduction sets the tone for the entire research paper and provides valuable information to orient the reader to your specific research topic. APA states that this section "presents the specific problem under study and describes the research strategy" (2010, p. 27). Even more basically, Mertler and Charles note that "introductions specify the topic and tell why it merits attention" (2008, p. 173). For our purposes, the introduction should include a general overview of the current research project, relevant background information, importance of the topic, the purpose statement, and specific research questions that will be addressed.

General Overview of the Research Project

An introduction must set the stage for what is to follow by providing a sketch of the central concerns of the study. The challenge in writing the introduction is to be both compelling and concise. The general overview can be thought of as the written version of a 30-second oral response you would give to someone inquiring, "So, what's your project about?" Thomas (2005) suggests that you adopt a reader's perspective in this opening section and pose yourself this question: "In the report's early pages, by what phrasing and in what sequence, would I—if I were a reader—most easily grasp the purpose of the research and understand, in general, how the project was carried out?" (p. 22).

Relevant Background Information

Context is critical in action research. Specific venues and settings both give rise to and shape the research. Since action research by its very nature is localized, it is incumbent on you to describe your school, parish, or diocese. You need to paint a vibrant picture for your reader, detailing the most important and relevant information regarding your school community. What are the top three important pieces of information that the reader will need to know about your school community? You may describe relevant historical elements of your school community (e.g., shift from religious to lay leadership), your own role in the educational setting (e.g., teacher, principal, development director), or organizational structures in the school (e.g., block or traditional scheduling, grade level groups, extended day). That type of detail informs the reader of important contextual information and provides insight into how applicable your work might be to their own. In fact, through this section, "readers will first become engaged in the study being reported and make decisions about whether and to what extent this study is likely to contain findings that are seen as reliable or can be transferred to wider settings" (James, Milenkiewicz, & Bucknam, 2008, p. 181). Complete the exercise in Mini-Lab 3.1 to identify salient and relevant background information to include in your introduction.

Mini-Lab 3.1: Relevant Background Information

Relevant background information on your school, parish, or local community can be a helpful way to include additional context for your action research project. Consider 3-5 elements of your school or parish that provide important insight into the community.

Highlighting Importance

Another objective of the introduction is to clearly articulate why your topic/issue is important (Hendricks, 2006). As Suter notes, this is your response to the critic who asks, "Who cares?" (2006, p. 407). That is, while "the rationale for your planned research may be obvious to you, many readers might wonder about its importance when put in the context of more pressing issues in education" (p. 407). Therefore, it is imperative to marshal evidence that helps make the case that a specific educational issue does exist in your school community, that it is worthy of research, and that you have a novel or compelling response to this issue that is particularly well-suited for action research. Ask yourself, how does my research topic relate to larger issues in education or the Church? Moreover, as teachers and leaders in Catholic schools you will likely draw on the teaching and traditions of the Church to contextualize your research. For example, Fierro (2008) found inspiration in Catholic Social Teaching to highlight the importance of restructuring reading instruction at the elementary school level to better meet the needs of a significant percentage of English language learners (ELL) in his school.

In the previous chapter, specifically Mini-Lab 2.3, you engaged in this initial thought process when you wrote your research problem. The introduction is where those thoughts are elaborated and expanded. An engaging quote, a provocative statistic, or a case example not only describes the problem, but signifies its importance. Such evidence exists in many forms, but some of the more common that you might draw upon might be standardized test scores, teacher surveys, parent feedback, classroom observations, accreditation results, and student feedback. Careful attention to evidence selection is warranted, making sure that your claims are based on defined sources and represent not just opinion or hearsay.

Statement of Purpose

Perhaps the most important deliverable of the introduction is a purpose statement: delineating the goal of your action research. Research purposes may be to address "a gap in knowledge, an uncertainty, conflicting research findings, or a disturbing trend" (Suter, 2006, p. 406). Be as direct as possible. Examples include:

- "The purpose of this action research was to evaluate the process, implementation, and impact of a newly structured advisory system on conditionally accepted students in the ninth grade" (Kmack, 2008, p. 137).
- "This study aimed to investigate if learners embraced collaborative learning and peer assessment by participating in various online and face-to-face activities in addition to attending formal lectures" (Ng, 2008, p. 102).
- "Specifically, the study seeks to determine whether students who completed some or all of the St. Edward [Pre-Engineering Program] curriculum are more likely to major in engineering in college than the national averages, and the degree to which they are prepared for successful college engineering study" (O'Linn & Scott, 2008, p. 240).

A secondary function of the purpose statement is to continue the process of narrowing and refining your research topic from the general overview in the introduction to the specific research questions that follow. The purpose statement is the one place in the introduction where you combine the importance and context of your specific research topic in a single sentence.

Research Questions

Recalling Figure 2.1 (p. 14), stating your research questions represents the culminating step in the narrowing from broad (a research topic) to specific (particular research inquiries). A research question—"defined as the fundamental question inherent in the research topic under investigation"—guides the research process (Mertler, 2009, p. 73). Make sure that the research question is aligned with your problem statement, and later, your literature review (Hendricks, 2006). Quantitative questions typically fall into three categories: (a) descriptive questions seek to understand by asking "how much?," "how often?," or "what changes over time or different situations?"; (b) predictive questions discern what variables or activities are predictive of particular outcomes; and (c) causal questions, like "does a change in x lead to a change in y?," seek to understand whether varying one construct leads to change in another (Johnson & Christensen, 2004, p. 78). Here are three examples of school-based action research questions:

- "Will ability grouping across classrooms and grade levels for reading instruction have a positive impact on reading achievement for kindergarten students?" (Duncan, 2008).
- "What is the impact of including native Spanish-speaking ELL students as teacher assistants into my beginning-level Spanish classes?" (Hanson, 2007, p. 261).
- "How do first graders learn number facts?" (Sanford, 2004, p. 38).

Summary Guidelines for Developing Your Introduction

While your introduction is unique to the research context and chosen topic, there are some standard approaches to crafting this section. Ideally, as we reviewed, the following elements should be addressed in the introduction:

- General introduction to research topic
- Relevant school background information
- Purpose of the research
- Research questions or hypotheses to be addressed

The content and structure of your introduction should reflect the specific research questions and methodology of your study. Figure 3.1 is a template to use as a guide when constructing your introduction outline.

Figure 3.1   Outline for Constructing the Introduction

Introduction

1. General Introduction

    a. What is the school-based issue you will be addressing?

    b. What relevant background information about your school (e.g., charism, personnel, policy, etc.) orients the reader to your research topic?

2. Importance of the Study

    a. Why is the study important?

    b. What new insights, professional practices, or policy changes are likely to occur because of your research?

    c. To whom is this information important or relevant?

3. Purpose Statement

    a. What is your specific approach to addressing the educational issue or problem?

    b. Example: The purpose of this action research project was to...

4. Research Questions

    a. What are the specific research questions you will explore in your action research project?

        i. Example: (Quantitative): Do parishioners with school-age children value the school differently than parishioners without school-age children?

        ii. Example: (Qualitative): What reasons do parents provide for enrolling their children in Saint Michael School? What do stakeholders at Saint Michael School and Parish identify as primary concerns or issues regarding the impact of school consolidation on their school and parish community?

Literature Review

The literature review is an extension and expansion of the research topic and general themes presented in the introduction. APA (2010) does not distinguish between the introduction section and literature review. However, for the purposes of your AR report, the literature review will be a new section detailing a written summary of research and scholarly reports directly related to your specific research topic.

What It Is

A literature review is a thoughtful and systematic consideration of sources—journal articles, books, monographs, summaries, conference papers, reports—related to your topic (Gay, Mills, & Airasian, 2009). The literature review sets your particular topic in a theoretical context and "helps tie your action research topic to what others have said and done before you" (Johnson, 2008, p. 75). Mertler and Charles (2008) offer a three part purpose for the literature review: "a) determine whether studies already exist similar to the one you propose to do; b) possibly obtain guidance for the investigation of your topic; and c) establish a point of departure or a platform on which to build your research" (p. 174).

A well-crafted literature review is a condensed, orderly, and concise summary of the knowledge base surrounding your topic. According to APA, the literature review should include only "relevant related literature...do not feel compelled to include an exhaustive historical account" (2010, p. 28). Developing the literature review actually positions you to be a more competent researcher. Johnson notes that "you do not have to reinvent the wheel; instead, you can use the insights of others to make your research more efficient and effective" (2008, p. 75). In organizing and producing the literature review, you gain a commanding knowledge of a focused topical area; moreover, through the review you demonstrate your competency—indeed a nascent expertise—around the major issues relevant to your topic. Beyond reviewing research on the major operative constructs relative to your topic and their interrelationship, literature reviews bring to a fine point considerations of the remaining unaddressed or unsolved questions regarding your topic, "what modes of investigation now seem appropriate, and why the problem remains viable" (Locke, Silverman, & Spirduso, 2004, p. 183).

Compiling the Literature Review

The literature review is not meant to be a fully comprehensive presentation of all empirical studies related to your research topic. Johnson and Christensen instruct that "the review is not exhaustive but cites only studies that are directly pertinent to place the current study in the context of prior work and to give an appropriate history and recognition of the work of others" (2004, pp. 532-533). Most essentially, the construction of the literature review is an exercise in integration and synthesis. More than simply compiling and listing one study after another, an effective literature review provides a synthesis of relevant research materials in a manner that is easily accessible and understandable to the reader.

Creating this synthesis of relevant studies typically proceeds in a fairly straightforward, stepwise fashion. First, if you have not already done so, refining your research topic is an important step in preparation for the literature review; clarity of topic will allow you to narrow your search and identify more relevant studies. You may wish to make a preliminary list of key words in Mini-Lab 3.2 that describe the components of your study.

Mini-Lab 3.2: Key Words for Literature Review

Constructing a literature review can be a daunting task. To help focus your search and identify the literature base most appropriate for your topic, brainstorm a list of key words. List the top five words or phrases that come to mind when you think about your research topic. Alternatively, explain your research to a friend or colleague and ask him or her to identify a few key words, too.

Second, you must locate relevant sources, often through extensive library and Internet searches. Most likely you will use library-based databases such as Academic Search Premier, Education Abstracts Full Text, Educational Research Information Center (ERIC), PsychINFO, or Web of Science. Depending on the capabilities of your academic library, many of these search engines can be utilized simultaneously via a single portal. You have the ability to search by keyword, authors, and even delimit the search parameters to include particular time periods (e.g., only articles within the last 10 years). These search tools will either provide a link to a full text copy of the source, an html document, or a full bibliographic citation if the source must be retrieved from the library's physical holdings.

Third, the obtained sources should be perused and evaluated. It is important to note a caveat at this point that your literature sources are not created equal. Some are simply better, higher quality, or more relevant than others, and you need some criteria to make such discernments. To evaluate sources, consider the following points about any particular research source:

- **Topic relevance:** Is the literature on the same topic as your proposed study?
- **Individual and site relevance:** Does the literature examine the same individuals in the same context/sites you want to study?
- **Problem relevance:** Does the literature examine the same research problem as you propose in your study?
- **Accessibility relevance:** Is a copy of the literature available through the library or can it be downloaded from a Web site?

Consider the source of the source. Generally speaking, primary sources (e.g., journal articles, scholarly books, technical reports, dissertations, etc.) should be more represented than secondary sources (e.g., encyclopedias, handbooks of research, research reviews, etc.). Also, sources that are peer-reviewed or refereed carry more weight than those that are not. For example, Creswell (2008) advocates a literature review priority system: refereed journal articles; non-refereed journal articles; books; conference papers, dissertations, and theses; and non-reviewed articles posted to Web sites. Use Mini-Lab 3.3 to organize your sources.

Mini-Lab 3.3: Organizing Your Sources

Once you have identified and collected sources for your literature review, take some time to "consider the source." List the number of sources you have from each of the categories outlined above. If your categories are unbalanced, especially if you have too few primary or high quality sources, you may have to continue your search.

Primary Sources: Journal articles, scholarly books, technical reports, dissertations/ theses

Secondary Sources: Encyclopedias, handbooks of research, textbooks, popular periodicals/newsprint

Fourth, for each of your relevant sources, you should summarize the piece through your own note taking. It is useful to create your own organizational system to catalog key information from sources such as full bibliographic information, major research questions, the methods used, and the key findings (Creswell, 2008; Mertler & Charles, 2008). Note taking helps to avoid plagiarism and encourages you to cultivate your own mastery of the material.

Fifth, looking across all of the relevant studies that you have unearthed and summarized, what are the major or most salient themes? Use this "pre-writing" phase to discern what the major themes are and how you will organize and address each of them. Holly, Arhar, and Kasten (2009) recommend that you "present what you've learned in chunks, depending on how things fit together" (p. 252). Traditional outlining—using headings and sub-headings to denote major literature categories and important sub-levels—is indispensible at this stage. Some may prefer a more graphic approach, using idea mapping (Creswell, 2008; Hendricks, 2006) to visually cluster major literature themes and their sub-components (see Figure 3.2).

Creswell offers guidance on the mechanics of assembling the literature review and describes the thematic method, which groups multiple studies or reports into themes addressed in your action research project (e.g., differentiated instruction, student assessment, etc.). For example, in reviewing the literature on school-based technology programs, Bayer (2008) grouped extant literature in the subcategories of school-based laptop initiatives, student motivation and attitudes toward learning, academic performance and quality of student work, teacher methodology and instruction, followed by a summary of each section and the implications for the current study.

Figure 3.2   Idea Mapping for Your Literature Review

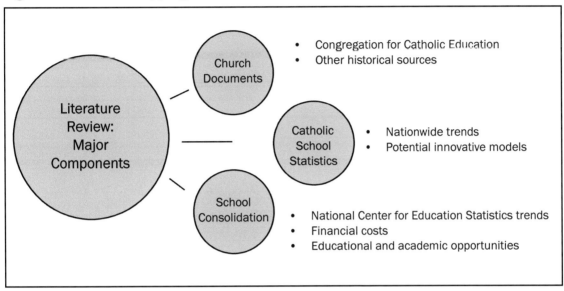

Another approach is a study-by-study method, which offers a detailed review of several studies, citing specific information about the method and findings for each. The review may often be organized chronologically across a particular topic or series of studies. Whichever way you organize your literature review, be sure to define terms that may be unfamiliar. "You can assume the reader has a general knowledge of education ideas and vocabulary but may not know terms that are unique to a particular specialty area" (Suter, 2006, pp. 407-408).

Another important component of the literature review for Catholic school teachers and leaders is the synthesis and integration of traditions, teachings, and specific documents of the Church. Like other sources that inform and shape your study, these Church resources can add depth, context, and focus to your AR project. For example, Frazier (2008) framed her research on Catholic schools' access to federal educational services by citing papal encyclicals and letters from the United States Conference of Catholic Bishops. Frazier contextualized school efforts to serve children with disabilities according to the fundamental principle that "each person is made in the image of God, which demands respect for the dignity of each individual, particularly disabled children, who are some of the most vulnerable and underserved in society" (p. 70). As you can discern from this excerpt, Catholic Social Teaching provided the orienting context and framework for Frazier's research; it is an integral component of her action research project and report.

Summary Guidelines for Developing the Literature Review

The content and structure of your literature review should reflect the specific topic, context, research questions, and methodology of your study. Figure 3.3 presents a general template to use as a guide when developing your literature review. Remember, often novice researchers consider the literature review process to be a daunting—perhaps even intimidating—proposition. Mertler and Charles (2008) concede that

> writing the literature review is quite honestly not an easy task. There is no "recipe" for developing the actual written review. It will likely take several iterations of written drafts, perhaps organizing and reorganizing the analysis of your related literature. (p. 87)

With that in mind, realize that there is a developmental process to crafting your literature review. Revise and reorganize as needed and solicit the input of outside readers to challenge and clarify your thinking and writing.

Figure 3.3   Outline for Constructing the Literature Review

Literature Review

1. Literature Review Introduction
    a. Engaging quote or statistic
    b. Advanced organizer or general overview of the scope of the literature review

2. First Research Theme
    a. General overview of first research theme
    b. Discussion of major findings or implications of this group of studies

3. Second Research Theme
    a. General overview of second research theme
    b. Discussion of major findings or implications of this group of studies

4. General Conclusion
    a. Brief summary of major issues, findings, and implications of the literature
    b. Brief commentary on the importance of and connection to your specific research

Conclusion

Describing the problem, the research context, and the current knowledge base as it relates to your topic is the firm foundation that supports the rest of your action research. As a self-check, once you have completed the introduction and the literature review, Locke et al. (2004) encourage you to consider whether the reader will be able to answer the following two most basic questions: What is the report about? How does the study fit into what is already known? Ask your colleagues to assist you in a peer review of your introduction and literature review through Mini-Lab 3.4.

Mini-Lab 3.4: Peer Review of Introduction and Literature Review

As you write and revise your literature review, exchange it with friends or colleagues and ask for their feedback. Have them consider the following questions:

1. Are the primary components of the literature review salient enough that you could summarize them after reading this section of the paper?
2. Do the components of the literature review address major components of the research questions?
3. At the end of the literature review, is it obvious how the proposed action research project responds to and fits with existing knowledge and research on the topic?

Action Research in Action:
Introduction and Literature Review

Stakeholder Perspectives on the Consolidation of Saint Michael Catholic School

The landscape of Catholic schools has changed quite dramatically in the past 50 years; personnel, student enrollment, and the overall number of schools have experienced marked change. At their zenith in the 1960s, Catholic schools enrolled over 5 million students in nearly 13,000 schools across the United States. These schools were staffed and led almost entirely by women and men religious. For the 2009-2010 academic year, Catholic schools enrolled approximately 2.12 million students in just over 7,000 K-12 schools—less than half of the schools and students from just five decades ago (McDonald & Schultz, 2010). What's more, these schools are now almost entirely staffed by lay women and men.

Saint Michael Catholic School has not been invulnerable to the enrollment and staffing issues affecting Catholic schools nationally. Situated in the urban center of a large, Midwestern city, Saint Michael School and Parish has experienced significant change since its founding over 130 years ago.... [section continues].

Purpose Statement

The purpose of this action research project was to explore stakeholder perceptions of the proposed school consolidation plan.

Research Questions

The major research questions considered in this action research project were:

1. What do stakeholders at Saint Michael School and Parish identify as primary concerns or issues regarding the impact of school consolidation on their school and parish community?

2. What is the 5-year enrollment trend at Saint Michael School?

Literature Review

With a net loss of over 1,000 Catholic schools in the last decade alone, Catholic schools are increasingly faced with important decisions about consolidation and closure (McDonald

PERSPECTIVES ON CATHOLIC SCHOOL CONSOLIDATION   4

& Schultz, 2010). The following literature review addresses three primary themes to better
understand the foundation of and contemporary challenges facing Catholic schools: Church
documents on Catholic education, Catholic school statistics, and school consolidation.

    Church documents on Catholic education. Catholic schools in the United States
comprise a unique context wherein in the sacred and secular commingle. As such, Catholic
schools are the "privileged environment in which Christian education is carried out"
(Congregation for Catholic Education, 1998, para. 11). Since the Third Plenary Council of
Baltimore in 1884, Catholic religious and laypersons have relied on the parish school to serve
as the primary provider of this privileged educational environment (Walch, 2003). In response
to the perceived prejudice and mistreatment of Catholic children attending the Common public
school, U.S. Bishops encouraged all parishes to build schools, and all Catholic parents to send
their children to these new parish schools (McCluskey, 1964). Walch (2003) stated,

      Catholic parents had a moral responsibility to provide for the spiritual lives of their

      children, and the best means of providing that spiritual life was through parish schools.

      Catholic parents were never *required* to send their children to parish schools until 1884,

      but not to do so was to incur the displeasure of the organized church. (p. 32)

Though the need for and importance of an education rooted in our Catholic faith has not
dissipated, the one-parish-one-school model established over 200 years ago has waned in recent
decades.... [section continues].

    Catholic school statistics. The most recent annual report from the National Catholic
Educational Association (NCEA; McDonald & Schultz, 2010) indicated that in the last year
alone 174 Catholic schools were closed or consolidated. Accounting for new school openings
in the same time period (24), there was a net loss of 150 schools. Over the past six decades,
the net effect of school consolidation and closing has yielded a loss of over 5,000 schools and
3.10 million students (McDonald & Schultz, 2010). These trends have empowered leaders in

the Church and educational research to wonder what new and innovative models might address these dramatic changes in our Catholic educational system (Golway, 2007; Hamilton, 2008; McLaughlin, O'Keefe, & O'Keeffe, 1996). Despite growing evidence that Catholic schools provide civic and financial benefits at the local and national level, many face consolidation and closure (Brinig & Garnett, 2009; Green, 2011).... [section continues].

     School consolidation. School consolidation is not a new phenomenon in the United States. Over the past seven decades, average public school enrollment has increased from roughly 100 students per school to 500 students per school (National Education Statistics, 2010). Economies of scale (e.g., leveraging buying power of larger school districts and schools) and reduced administrative costs (e.g., fewer building- and district-level administrators) are often cited as the benefits of consolidating schools in states and school districts across the U.S. (Ash, 2007; Dodson & Garrett, 2004). There are costs associated with consolidation, too. Since 1930, the percentage of school-age children who ride the bus to school has increased from 10% to 60% (Kileen & Sipple, 2000). In addition to the financial costs, a growing body of research indicates that smaller schools may actually serve students better academically and provide more educational opportunities (Lee & Smith, 1997). Lee and Loeb (2000) stated that "a crucial element of any school's structure is the number of students enrolled, that is, the size of the school," which can have an impact on teachers and students alike (p. 4).... [section continues].

     A tension exists between the centrality of Catholic schools to the Church's education apostolate, and the financial and demographic realities that threaten the feasibility of many parish schools. While the canon of official Church documents extols the prominence and value of Catholic education, the number of U.S. Catholic schools has been in precipitous decline for the past five decades. School consolidation is one option that increasing numbers of parishes and schools are considering as an alternative to school closure. Though a promising option, school consolidation is not without complications and concessions.

4

Method

The method section is a departure from the contextualizing of your action research set forth in the introduction and literature review. In this section you will provide a detailed description of how your study was actually conducted. The American Psychological Association (APA) states "a complete description of the methods used enables the reader to evaluate the appropriateness of your methods and the reliability and validity of your results" (2010, p. 29). The method section, therefore, functions as both a blueprint for your proposed research and a record of activity that demonstrates a clear connection between your research questions and your research protocol—between what you want to know and how you set about getting answers. Furthermore, an effective method section describes in detail the major procedural components of the study without being overly narrative or verbose.

There are several essential components to the method section of your AR report: participants, instruments/materials, and design and procedure. This chapter will provide an overview of each of these major components and a series of mini-labs and examples to assist you in the development of your research method section.

AR Insight

We have found that articulating a research plan in the method section often challenges action researchers to consider the larger implications of their research projects. What does your selection of participants say about the value of community? How has the design of your research project promoted solidarity or reflected the dignity of all persons? As you grapple with these questions stemming from important methodological considerations, be open to the concurrent connection with our Catholic faith and Catholic Social Teaching. As such, each component in the method section provides an opportunity for you to highlight how practitioners enact social justice when they engage real world issues through action research.

Participants

Nearly all applied educational research involves participants—human beings from a target population who will participate in your research. Although you may already have an idea of who you will study (e.g., teachers in my building) and why you will study them (e.g., precisely because they are conveniently located in my building), these decisions will have implications for the kind of data you receive and the claims you are ultimately able to make with that data. In fact, the participants in your study are only one part of a larger exercise in sampling.

As part of the research process, sampling is concerned with selecting units of analysis that are representative of the population under study. This definition requires some unpacking of key terms.

First, unit of analysis refers to the level at which data are collected in a given study (Creswell, 2008). For example, the focus of a study may be at the individual, classroom, school, or diocesan level. Selecting a unit of analysis is linked to the research question that you want to answer: Are you interested in changes in individual students' test scores? Are you interested in comparing the test scores of two fourth grade classrooms in the same building? Are you situating the performance of your school in contrast to others in the same city or diocese? Your response to questions like these dictates the appropriate unit of analysis for your action research project.

Second, once a unit of analysis is selected, the researcher must define the population from which these units will be sampled. Said another way, you must identify the overall group from which your participants will be selected. Let us assume that you want to survey school teachers who have taught 5 or fewer years in a Catholic school. In this example, teachers are the unit of analysis. All teachers who have taught 5 or fewer years in a Catholic school are the population since they are the overall group of individuals who share the same characteristic (Creswell, 2008).

You can see right away that it would not be feasible for you to survey each and every teacher with 5 or fewer years of teaching experience in all U.S. Catholic schools (i.e., the entire population). Therefore, you must define a reasonable target population or subset of the overall population. Mertens (1998) refers to this activity as defining the "experimentally accessible population...the list of people who fit the conceptual definition" (p. 255). The target or experimentally accessible population is also known as the sampling frame and effectively defines the boundaries of your population. All participants for your study will fit within the sampling frame or target population for your study (see Figure 4.1). In this example, a feasible target population might be all teachers with 5 or fewer years teaching in three dioceses across the country.

Finally, once you have defined your target population, you must select actual individuals to participate in your study. Selecting individuals from the target population yields the sample for your study. As it turns out, there are actually many

Figure 4.1   General Model of Sampling Procedures

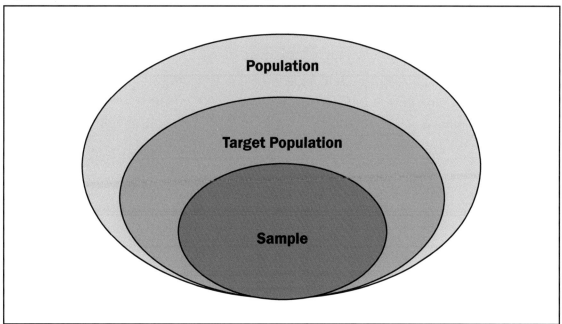

tried and true methods for systematically generating a sample. These methods are roughly divided into two general categories: probabilistic and non-probabilistic sampling techniques (Henry, 1990, 1998). The following paragraphs explore some of the more common probabilistic and non-probabilistic sampling techniques.

AR Insight

As teachers and leaders engaged in applied research in your school, community, and diocese, your personal relationships and professional connections are an excellent resource for gaining access to stakeholder groups and institutions—participants for your AR project. Developing these relationships with colleagues, and being careful not to exert undue pressure to participate, will promote collaborative working relationships that will extend well beyond any one research project.

Probabilistic Sampling Techniques

Probabilistic sampling techniques "have the distinguishing characteristic that each unit in the population has a known, nonzero probability of being selected for the sample. To have this characteristic, a sample must be selected through a random mechanism" (Henry, 1998, p. 106). Simply put, probabilistic sampling assures that each participant has an equal and unbiased chance to end up in the sample. Here are some common examples of probabilistic sampling techniques.

Simple random sampling. Simple random sampling is one of the most common forms of probabilistic sampling. As the name suggests, the process is quite straightforward and simple. When conducting simple random sampling, researchers typically assign a number to all potential participants in the target population (i.e., teachers with 5 or fewer years teaching in Catholic schools from three dioceses). Researchers will then consult a table of random numbers, moving through the list in some form or fashion matching the number from the target population with the numbers generated from the table of random numbers. Each matched number represents one individual in the study sample. This process is repeated until the researcher has selected a sufficient number of participants for the study.

Systematic sampling. Systematic sampling is a modification of simple random sampling wherein researchers select every n^{th} individual from their list. For example, a researcher may have a list of all teachers with 5 or fewer years of teaching experience in Catholic schools from three dioceses across the United States. Knowing that they want to survey 25% of the teachers, the researcher may then proceed, from any point in the list, to select every fourth teacher for the study sample.

Stratified sampling. Stratified sampling is really a hybrid version of simple random sampling. With stratified random sampling, the researcher first divides the target population by some variable of interest (e.g., gender, years of experience, teaching discipline). This division is not done haphazardly; stratified sampling is undertaken when there are important features or ratios within the target population that the researcher wants to maintain within the sample. Once this division or stratification is complete, researchers then randomly select participants from these new groups to appoint to the study sample.

Non-Probabilistic Sampling Techniques

Non-probabilistic sampling is the second general category of sampling techniques used in social science research. Non-probabilistic sampling differs from probabilistic sampling in that "selective judgments play a role in sample selection" (Henry, 1998, p. 104). The array of non-probabilistic techniques requires researchers to make decisions about participants based on criteria such as availability, interest, and consent—decisions that require some level of input from the researcher and the participants. Here are a few of the more common non-probabilistic sampling techniques.

Convenience sampling. Convenience sampling is a process of choosing participants based on their availability or willingness to participate in the study. This may sound like an easy way out of the more rigorous demands of random sampling, but actually has an important function in action research. It is quite possible that you are not interested in teachers with 5 or fewer years of teaching experience in any Catholic school, but are interested in all teachers in your school. In this case, a sample of teachers at your school who were able to complete the requirements of your study would comprise the convenience sample. There are some important limitations to convenience sampling—you may not be able to generalize your findings to the larger population of teachers. However, as was stated before, this may not be the focus of your research in the first place.

Snowball sampling. Snowball sampling is a variation of convenience sampling. Imagine the snowball rolling down the hill, growing along the way as it collects more and more snow. This is essentially how snowball sampling works. You begin by asking an individual or group of individuals to participate in the study and, in turn, ask them to also invite or provide you with the name and contact information of friends or colleagues who fit the description of participants you are hoping to attract. The primary limitation with this method is that the selection criteria are effectively in the hands of the primary participants who are asking others to participate as well. Said another way, you are not quite sure who will end up in your sample. The trade off is that you may get greater access to some participants because their friend or colleague is asking them to participate, and not some researcher they may not know well.

Purposeful sampling. Purposeful sampling is the general term that is often used to describe myriad qualitative sampling techniques (Creswell, 2008; see Table 4.1). When using purposeful sampling techniques, researchers choose specific individuals or sites to study because they exemplify salient features of the phenomenon of interest. More than for their convenience or availability, these individuals or institutions are selected precisely because the researcher believes they will make an important and unique contribution to the questions of interest.

Table 4.1

Overview of Common Purposeful Sampling Techniques

Technique	General description
Maximal variation	Multiple individuals or institutions with key trait differences (e.g., age, experience, location, etc.)
Extreme cases	Outliers at each end of the spectrum (e.g., programs that have succeeded and failed)
Critical cases	The essential, sometimes dramatic, example of a phenomenon of interest (e.g., the founding school of a new network of urban, private schools)

I hope you are able to see that, at the end of the day, the complex decisions regarding your specific sample ultimately "depend on the goals and practicality of the research" (Henry, 1998, p. 101). Appropriate and well-executed sampling procedures will allow you to cut through some of the chatter (i.e., see beyond the opinions provided only by the loudest or most persistent members of a given population) and ensure that you are accessing the most complete, accurate, and important information to answer your questions of interest.

As a final check, be sure to consider important and relevant groups of individuals you may have inadvertently overlooked. Are there traditionally marginalized populations who would have important insights into your research questions? Can you reach out to these groups and engage them in your research? Not only is it possible that these individuals and groups of individuals will provide a unique contribution to your research, your efforts to include them may extend beyond sound sampling procedure and manifest tenets of Catholic Social Teaching through preferential option for the poor and marginalized (Frabutt, Holter, & Nuzzi, 2008). Complete Mini-Lab 4.1 to determine your sampling procedures.

Mini-Lab 4.1: Sampling Procedures

Think about your own research topic and the specific research questions you articulated in chapter 3 when answering the following questions:

1. What is the unit of analysis for your action research project?
2. Define the population and target population.
3. What sampling procedures best fit your research questions and target population?
4. What individuals or groups of individuals might you be overlooking as you define your action research target population and sample?

Once you have identified your sample, you will have to introduce your participants to the reader. The design of your research (which will be discussed later in this chapter) will determine what kind and how much information you include about your participants. But do not go overboard. Demographic information about participants should "describe the groups as specifically as possible, with particular emphasis on characteristics that may have bearing on the interpretation of results" (APA, 2010, p. 29). For example, in a largely quantitative study you might include the average age or gender distribution of all respondents. In a small, qualitative study you might provide a fuller description, a brief narrative even, of the two or three participants you interviewed. Here are a few examples of the kinds of information you may want to include about the participants in your study:

- Who are they? What are some key demographic variables of interest (e.g., gender, age, years experience or affiliation, etc.)?
- How many participated in total? How many are included in relevant sub-groups?
- In what context or environment did you find them (e.g., school, parish, home, etc.)?

Remember, there is no magic number or formula to predict the precise number of participants for every study. The number and type of participants you will need for a valid and reliable study will depend largely on the kind of action research project you are conducting. There are effective formulas and protocols for determining power and sensitivity of specific sample sizes (e.g., Cohen, 1988; Lipsey, 1990), and many texts that provide general "rules of thumb" when it comes to determining optimal sample sizes (Borg & Gall, 1989; Creswell, 2008; Fowler, 2009), but covering statistical power and sensitivity is beyond the scope of this text. Furthermore, action researchers rarely conduct the kinds of randomized experimental research with the freedom to choose sample sizes. You are likely constrained by the number of students in a classroom or building, the number of teachers in a diocese, and so on. And that is not a bad thing. It is precisely because of these idiosyncratic realities in applied educational research that we recommend a more organic approach to determining sample size. In the words of Henry (1998), "the researcher needs a bridge to connect the goals of the study with the practical considerations of conducting research. Sampling methods, or the methods by which members of a population are selected for a study, provide that bridge" (p. 101).

Instruments and Materials

The function of this component of the method section is to introduce and describe the measurement instruments (e.g., surveys, interview protocols, etc.) and materials (e.g., new math curriculum, professional development program, etc.) that were used in your study. The *Publication Manual of the American Psychological Association* refers to this sub-section as as "measures and covariates" and recommends the title "materials and procedures" (APA, 2010, p. 31). However, for our purposes and for your action research report, we will use the title "Instruments and Materials." As such, the information in this section will provide a clearer picture of the primary tools and resources used to conduct your research.

Instruments
Measurement instruments are the tests, questionnaires, survey items, interview protocols, focus group questions—really any and all forms of assessment—you will

use to collect specific data from your participants. Before you choose your instruments, it is helpful to focus on exactly what kinds of data you are after. Developing "operational definitions" is a helpful step in articulating your variables of interest (see Figure 4.2 for an overview of creating operational definitions). An operational definition is "the specification of how you will define and measure the variable(s) in your study" (Creswell, 2008, p. 160). For example, for the purposes of your research, you may define the variable "school engagement" as the number of hours spent in non-required extracurricular school activities (e.g., sports, debate or speech club, student volunteer organizations, etc). Your definitions may be the same as or different than definitions found in the literature—there are many variations of even the simplest and most straightforward variables—and that is why being certain about what they mean for you and your study is so important.

Figure 4.2   Operationalizing Variables of Interest

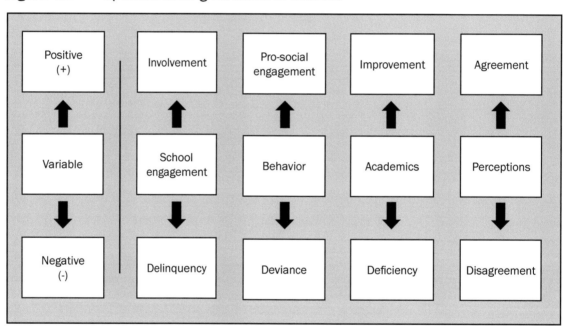

Much of the work you did earlier to develop a research topic and articulate specific research questions is congruent with and advances the task of articulating operational definitions. These precise definitions for key variables will produce search terms and decision rules as you seek and evaluate a variety of measures with myriad formats and methods of delivery. However, before you begin that search it is helpful to brainstorm (see Mini-Lab 4.2) some general ideas for the kinds of measures you are seeking.

Now that you have a general idea of the kinds of instruments you will use, you can begin to search for them. Creswell (2008) advises that when selecting a measurement instrument you can "develop one yourself, locate one and modify it, or locate one and use it in its entirety" (p. 167). For our purposes, we will invert that list and first discuss using instruments in their entirety and then entertain the possibility of modifying or creating measurement instruments.

Mini-Lab 4.2: Measurement Match

Consider the key variables associated with your research questions (e.g., math achievement, stakeholder awareness of school activities, parent attitudes regarding school consolidation, etc.) and the kinds of instruments you might employ to access that information (e.g., standardized test scores, Web-based survey instrument, individual interviews, etc.). Be as specific as possible regarding the focus of your variables, and the content and format of the measurement instruments.

Even if you end up modifying or creating your own instrument, it is a good idea to start by perusing the literature for existing measures. Perhaps you will find the ideal measure for your study; at the very least you will have a general understanding of the multiple content and format options available to you. Journal articles are a great place to begin this search. In fact, as you were collecting information for the literature review you likely encountered several studies that referenced or summarized measures applicable to your own variables of interest. Sufficient bibliographic information should accompany these descriptions—either in text or in the reference section—so that you can track down the original author or publisher of the specific instrument. Better still, some articles will include the entire instrument in the appendix. As a gesture of professional courtesy, you might consider sending a brief e-mail to the primary contact asking permission to use their instrument.

A general search of library databases is another option for locating measurement instruments. Use the key words associated with your variables of interest or operational definitions to search databases such as ERIC, PsychINFO, and EBSCOhost. Sometimes simply entering key words (e.g., math achievement, school climate, parent perceptions of school) and the measurement format (e.g., survey, questionnaire, interview protocol) together in a general search window will produce many relevant sources.

Finally, consider searching commercially produced measurement instruments. Corporations such as Harcourt and PsychCorp Assessment (www.pearsonassess.com), Tests in Print (TIP; through the BUROS center at www.unl.edu/buros/), Educational Testing Services (ETS; www.ets.org), and many others provide comprehensive catalogues of a wide array of psychological and educational measurement instruments. There is a catch, though. Commercially produced instruments and tests are often expensive and available only to licensed or certified individuals. However, many companies offer access and discounts for students through a sponsoring professor with the appropriate credentials.

At this point it is worth noting, if not already obvious, that not all measurement instruments are created equal. There are a variety of factors that affect instrument quality, but for quantitative measures, reliability and validity are the two strongest and most commonly cited. So important are these factors that "data are useless if they are not accurate, valid, and reliable" (Bickman, Rog, & Hedrick, 1998, p. 20). The reliability of a measure indicates its ability to perform consistently over time and across situations. There are many ways to calculate reliability (e.g., test-retest reliability, inter-rater reliability, alternate or parallel forms reliability, etc.), but the most common is internal consistency reliability. Internal consistency reliability refers to the consistency or "similar functioning" of items within a given test or measure. A measure is said to have high internal consistency if individuals who complete the measure respond the same way to the same types of questions throughout the instrument. Cronbach's alpha is the most common measure of internal consistency reliability that can be calculated on a number of statistical programs (SPSS, SAS, etc.) with a range from 0 to 1 (Field, 2009). The closer the alpha is to 1, the higher the internal consistency. There is considerable debate over required alpha levels, but many social scientists will agree that an alpha above .70 is acceptable (Cortina, 1993; Cronbach, 1951; Grayson, 2004; Kline, 1999).

Validity is complementary to the measurement of reliability, and indicates the degree to which you are actually measuring what you say you are measuring. In other words, how do you know that you are actually measuring interest in mathematics and not some other variable like perception of school or general anxiety for that matter? Researchers address these important questions by demonstrating high levels of content, criterion, and construct validity.

Content validity is the degree to which items on an instrument represent the full range of possible questions about that topic or phenomenon. Valid measures of anger, for example, will include questions that address the behavioral, cognitive, and affective components of the emotion. A measure is said to have strong criterion validity when the scores or outcomes of the instrument are highly related to some other outcome variable. Standardized entrance exams such as the Graduate Record Examination (GRE), Law School Admission Test (LSAT), and Medical College Admission Test (MCAT) are common examples of criterion validity since they are designed to predict individual performance in advanced studies. Construct validity is the final and most complicated type of validity as it involves both statistical and practical analysis (Creswell, 2008). Consider construct validity as a subtle combination of reliability and the other validity indicators that, when effective, provides a convincing case that the particular measure is important and useful. In short, measurement instruments with high construct validity are relevant, interpretable, and provide important insight into a particular construct or phenomenon.

As you scour journals and databases for the ideal measurement instrument, be sure to look for the critical indicators of reliability and validity, but also consider additional criteria in Mini-Lab 4.3 for determining the quality of the instrument. The more affirmative answers you provide to these questions, the more likely it is that the instrument you are reviewing is right for your action research project.

Mini-Lab 4.3: Criteria for Choosing a Measurement Instrument

Criteria	Key questions
1. Relevance	Does the instrument measure your key variables of interest? Is it newly revised or updated? Is it cited often or used frequently in the literature?
2. Ease of use	Are the directions clearly stated and easy to understand? Does the format fit the content of the questions being asked? Is the language and length appropriate for your participants?
3. Interpretation	Do the questions match with the construct being measured? Will the response sets facilitate the kind of analysis you will run? Is there a rubric, handbook, or formula for scoring the instrument?
4. Cost	Is the instrument available at no cost in an academic journal? If there is a cost, is there a discount for students? Does the information yielded warrant the cost?

After searching through multiple sources to find the ideal instrument, it is quite possible that you are unable to locate one measure that includes the necessary features and assesses the precise variables germane to your action research project. Perhaps you find a valid and reliable measure of teacher efficacy that omits any focus on spirituality or sense of vocation. Or, there may be an exceptional reading assessment that is too advanced for the students in your study. In situations such as these you may need to modify an existing measure or create your own original instrument. Consider the following before you begin modifying existing instruments or creating your own:

1. Modifying measurement instruments in the public domain (i.e., published in an academic journal or report) is generally acceptable, but commercial measures cannot typically be used or even modified without express permission and payment.

2. Researchers who have created and published original measures are usually amenable to sharing their work and allowing modifications and revisions to the instrument. As mentioned above, be in contact with these authors as

they will likely want to know how the instrument worked for your specific population, suggestions you may have for further revisions, and they may also ask you to share the reliability analysis.

3. It is important to remember that when you modify the content or structure of an instrument, you can no longer count on the validity and reliability indicators as reported in the literature.

There are times, of course, when research questions and context are so specialized that no satisfactory measures exist to assess your questions of interest. When this is the case, you may need to create your own survey instrument or interview protocol. Delineating the requirements and procedures for the panoply of measurement instruments is beyond the scope of this text. However, below you will find a brief treatment of the measurement instruments most commonly used by practitioner researchers in our action research courses. Additionally, we have included a series of references for more information on these specific measurement instrument categories.

Surveys

Surveys are among the most common measurement instruments used by students in our action research courses. Mertler (2009) defines surveys as the "collective group of quantitative data-collection techniques that involve the administration of a set of questions or statements to a sample of people" (p. 117). Surveys are ubiquitous in American culture, appearing everywhere from popular magazines to news programs to social science research; yet, there are important guidelines to follow as you consider constructing your own survey instrument. Mertler (2009, p. 124) offers the following criteria:

- Each item should focus on a single idea or concept.
- Do not use too many questions or questions that are not necessary or repetitive.
- Keep the length of the survey brief and the reading level relatively easy; failing to do so often results in respondents not completing the instrument or providing you with inaccurate information.
- If you are designing a rating scale, you should keep the response scale consistent throughout the survey. Otherwise, respondents can become confused.
- Consider using both closed-response and open-ended items in order to realize the benefits of both.
- Do not use leading questions; a good survey or rating scale is one that contains objective items.

■   Always proofread your survey before you administer it to your participants. Also, pilot test your survey with colleagues who can provide insight and feedback on both the design and content of your instrument.

In general, a properly designed survey can be an excellent instrument for assessing "attitudes, perceptions, and opinions" of individuals on a wide variety of topics (Mertler, 2009, p. 124). However, special care must be taken to avoid survey items and instruments that lead the participant to a specific kind of response (leading) or yield data that are difficult to interpret (ambiguous). Maximizing advantages and minimizing the potential limitations of survey research can be achieved through careful attention to and construction of survey questions. Fowler (1998) recommends that "investing in the design and evaluation of questions is a best buy, one of the endeavors that is most likely to yield results in the form of better, more error-free data" (p. 343).

There are many excellent resources that will help you avoid some of the common mistakes and general disadvantages of survey measures, and maximize the potential of your survey instrument (see Figure 4.3). Additionally, consider how these recommendations are present in the sample survey in Figure 4.4.

Figure 4.3   Survey Resources

Converse, J. M., & Presser, S. (1986). *Survey questions: Handcrafting the standardized questionnaire.* Thousand Oaks, CA: Sage.

Dillman, D. (2007). *Mail and Internet surveys: The tailored design method* (2nd ed.). Hoboken, NJ: John Wiley & Sons.

Fanning, E. (2005). Formatting a paper-based survey questionnaire: Best practices. *Practical Assessment Research & Evaluation, 10*(12), 1-14.

Fowler, F. J. (2009). *Survey research methods* (4th ed.). Thouand Oaks, CA: Sage.

Schonlau, M., Fricker, R. D., & Elliot, M. N. (2002). *Conducting research surveys via email and the Web.* Santa Monica, CA: Rand.

Interview Protocols

Whether you are interviewing an individual (individual interview) or groups of individuals (focus groups), it is a good idea to have a plan or guide to structure your time. These guides are often called interview protocols and "contain instructions for the process of the interview, the questions to be asked, and space to take notes of responses from the interviewee(s)" (Creswell, 2008, p. 233). A well-designed interview protocol will provide important procedural information in addition to the questions you wish to ask the interviewee (see Figure 4.5 for resources).

Figure 4.4   Sample Survey Instrument

School Perceptions Survey—Saint Michael Parish and School

Dear Stakeholder,
Please answer the following questions to the best of your ability. Remember, there are no right or wrong answers and your responses are completely anonymous.

Affiliation with Saint Michael Parish and/or School (circle one):

Parishioner and parent of current Saint Michael Student   *Non-parishioner and parent of current Saint Michael Student*   *Parishioner without school-age children*   *Teacher at Saint Michael School*

Number of years affiliated in this capacity: _____

Please respond to the following questions by selecting the answer that is best for you; there are no right or wrong answers. Remember that your answers are anonymous and will only be reported as group averages.

1. Saint Michael School is an important ministry of Saint Michael Parish.

   Strongly Disagree   *Disagree*   *Agree*   *Strongly Agree*

2. There is a strong connection between Saint Michael Parish and School.

   Strongly Disagree   *Disagree*   *Agree*   *Strongly Agree*

3. The proposed school consolidation will be beneficial for Saint Michael Parish.

   Strongly Disagree   *Disagree*   *Agree*   *Strongly Agree*

4. Saint Michael School has sufficient resources to meet the needs of its students without consolidating.

   Strongly Disagree   *Disagree*   *Agree*   *Strongly Agree*

5. The proposed school consolidation will improve the quality of Catholic education in our community.

   Strongly Disagree   *Disagree*   *Agree*   *Strongly Agree*

General Comments:

Figure 4.5   Interview Protocol Resources

Creswell, J. W. (2008). *Educational research: Planning, conducting, and evaluating quantitative and qualitative research* (pp. 225-235). Upper Saddle River, NJ: Pearson.

Mertler, C. A. (2009). *Action research: Teachers as researchers in the classroom* (2nd ed., pp. 108-112). Thousand Oaks, CA: Sage.

Mertler, C. A., & Charles, C. M. (2008). *Introduction to educational research* (6th ed., pp. 135-136). Upper Saddle River, NJ: Pearson.

Interview protocols are used to structure three primary types of interviews presented here in descending level of structure: structured, semi-structured, and open-ended interviews (Creswell, 2008; Mertler, 2009). The protocol for a structured interview contains "a specific set of predetermined questions" that are asked in the same way to each and every interviewee (Mertler, 2009, p. 109). Structured interviews are designed for a consistent delivery of the exact same questions time after time. The semi-structured interview protocol combines some predetermined elements with room for follow-up or optional questions the interviewer can access at his or her discretion (see Figure 4.6). Finally, open-ended interview protocols contain minimal structure and a few broad questions. For example, an open-ended interview protocol for the Saint Michael School research example might include the question "What does Saint Michael School do well?"

Unlike close-ended or forced response survey questions, a well-designed interview protocol will allow stakeholders to respond to your questions of interest in their own voice and provide "detailed personal information" (Creswell, 2008, p. 226). There will be considerable time requirements for accessing this rich information (i.e., transcribing, cleaning, and coding the data) but careful design of your interview protocol will assist with this task and ensure you capture accurate and relevant data from your interviewees.

Observation Record and Data Checklist

The final category of common measures contains two instruments that are designed to help you identify and organize "behaviors, characteristics, skills, or other criteria that the researcher is interested in studying" (Mertler & Charles, 2008, p. 230). An observation record, sometimes referred to as fieldnotes, captures both general behaviors of the individual or group being observed (e.g., interpersonal interactions, dialogue) and your notes, commentary, or synthesis of those observed behaviors. Figure 4.7 provides an example of a general classroom observation record. In this example, the researcher would record important events or interactions in the left column, and then write his or her notes or commentary in the right column. This process could be repeated throughout the day or over a period of days.

The data checklist is a variation of the observation record and contains predetermined categories or specific items that the researcher will look for during an evaluation. Some social scientists assert that the checklist should be dichotomous (i.e., yes or no; Mertler, 2009), but there is considerable variation in the structure of these instruments. Figure 4.8 illustrates a classroom behavior checklist designed to assess the frequency of both pro- and antisocial interpersonal behavior in an elementary classroom. These instruments are designed to be quick and easy to use, however, the data they yield are typically not very detailed. As such, these instruments are great for capturing general information about a given context, individual, or group of individuals (i.e., classroom, classroom teacher, or a class of fifth grade students, respectively).

Figure 4.6   Sample Semi-Structured Interview Protocol

Location:
Date:
Interviewer:
Interviewee (name and position):

Purpose: Before the interview begins, remind the interviewee of the purpose of the research project, why they were selected, and how the data will be used. *The purpose of this research project is to examine ways in which Catholic schools can and should respond to the educational needs of Latino children and families. Your school has been selected because of your exemplary record for engaging the Latino community. As a stakeholder in this school community, I would like to hear your thoughts on how the school is able to do this so effectively. Your responses will remain confidential, but portions of your interview will be used in our final report. If you wish, we will change your name and the name of your school.*

Recording: Begin tape recorder after you have gone over the purpose of the study. For the record, state your name, the date, and ask participants to state their name.

Questions: Below are a series of potential interview and follow-up questions. Feel free to adjust the wording and order of these questions to respond to the specific interview you are conducting. Additionally, feel free to take notes or comment on any observations during the interview.

1. What is the history of the school?

    a. Can you point to a time when the school first began engaging and serving Latino children and families?

2. What does this school do well?

    a. What are you doing that other schools aren't?

3. Who are the key people behind the success of the school?

    a. Have some of these people left? When? Who are they?

4. Describe how you engage and celebrate the unique culture of the students and families at your school.

    a. Are there things/events outside of the school day that are especially important?

5. What are the key external factors that impact your success or challenges?

    a. What are the biggest challenges the school faces?

6. Describe the relationship between the parish and school.

    a. What is the role of the pastor?

7. What recommendations would you make to other schools seeking to serve Latino communities?

    a. What's the ONE most important factor from your perspective?

8. Do you have anything else you would like to add?

Additional Notes: Include any additional notes on the overall interview or specific elements of your interaction with the stakeholder.

Tips for Interviewers:
1. Make sure the interviewee knows who you are and why you are there.
2. Make sure you have a comfortable space free of distractions.
3. Feel free to use an icebreaker or conversation before actual interview begins.
4. Always ask permission to audiotape the interview.
5. Always thank the interviewee for their time.

Figure 4.7   Sample Classroom Observation Record

Observation Record—Elementary School Classroom

Location:
Date:
Start Time:
End Time:
Observer:

General activities during observation:

Time	Observed behaviors	Notes

Figure 4.8   Sample Data List

Classroom Behavior Checklist

Forgiveness Education Initiatives
University of Wisconsin—Madison

Name of School:
Name of Teacher:
Date of Observation:
Name of Observer:

Circle the number each time you observe the behaviors listed below. Columns are organized into groups of five (5) for ease of use and tabulation. Each number represents a single expression of the observed behavior.

Verbal Aggression	1 2 3 4 5	1 2 3 4 5	1 2 3 4 5	1 2 3 4 5	1 2 3 4 5
Proactive Aggression	1 2 3 4 5	1 2 3 4 5	1 2 3 4 5	1 2 3 4 5	1 2 3 4 5
Reactive Aggression	1 2 3 4 5	1 2 3 4 5	1 2 3 4 5	1 2 3 4 5	1 2 3 4 5
Stealing	1 2 3 4 5	1 2 3 4 5	1 2 3 4 5	1 2 3 4 5	1 2 3 4 5
Ignoring	1 2 3 4 5	1 2 3 4 5	1 2 3 4 5	1 2 3 4 5	1 2 3 4 5
Comforting	1 2 3 4 5	1 2 3 4 5	1 2 3 4 5	1 2 3 4 5	1 2 3 4 5
Instrumental Help	1 2 3 4 5	1 2 3 4 5	1 2 3 4 5	1 2 3 4 5	1 2 3 4 5
Kindness/Considerateness	1 2 3 4 5	1 2 3 4 5	1 2 3 4 5	1 2 3 4 5	1 2 3 4 5
Sharing/Donating	1 2 3 4 5	1 2 3 4 5	1 2 3 4 5	1 2 3 4 5	1 2 3 4 5
Making Amends	1 2 3 4 5	1 2 3 4 5	1 2 3 4 5	1 2 3 4 5	1 2 3 4 5

This brief overview of the most common measurement instruments is certainly not exhaustive (see Figure 4.9 for additional resources). In fact, as you consider the most appropriate measurement instrument for your AR project you may identify standardized tests (e.g., Iowa Test of Basic Skills), secondary data (e.g., school attendance data), or some combination of several different types. No doubt the measurement instrument you select will be relevant to your questions of interest and compatible with your research design (something we will discuss in the next section).

Figure 4.9   Observation Record and Data Checklist Resources

Creswell, J. W. (2008). *Educational research: Planning, conducting, and evaluating quantitative and qualitative research* (3rd ed., pp. 163-165, 220-225). Upper Saddle River, NJ: Pearson.

Johnson, A. P. (2008). *A short guide to action research* (3rd ed., pp. 83-90). Upper Saddle River, NJ: Pearson.

Mertler, C. A. (2008). *Action research: Teachers as researchers in the classroom* (2nd ed., pp. 106-109, 124-125). Thousand Oaks, CA: Sage.

When you finally choose your instruments, the next task is to present sufficient information about them so that the reader can evaluate the tools you are using to collect your data and, if they wish, replicate the assessment in their own AR project. Researchers typically include information about the structure of the instrument (i.e., number and type of questions, general format, etc.), validity and reliability measures if appropriate, a sample item in the text of the AR report (i.e., one question or category), and the entire instrument or suite of instruments in the appendix.

Materials

Materials are inclusive of all the resources, curricula, or special programs the participants use during your AR project. It is typical for the researcher to describe a sample activity, lesson, or event in the text of the AR report, and then direct the reader to a full overview of the lesson sequence or comprehensive program description in the appendix. You are not required to include any curriculum or special program in its entirety. Rather, present only enough information, illustrative quotes, or samples to sufficiently convey the content and structure of the materials. It is also possible that you do not have any materials to report in this section. If this is the case for your AR project, as it is for the Saint Michael School research example, do not include the *Materials* heading or any other information in this section of your AR report.

Design and Procedure

The design and procedure elements of your AR report have thus far informed nearly every component of your AR project. In non-research terms, these elements shape what your overall project looks like and how it was conducted. Moreover, you have likely been visualizing and articulating these elements as you discuss your research with friends and colleagues. As such, it may seem counterintuitive to address these essential elements after other components of the paper have been presented (i.e., participants, instruments and materials, etc.). Alas, APA format requires the design and procedure elements be placed here in the AR report, so we will address them in the same location in this text.

Consider how the design and procedure elements have affected your AR project by responding to the questions in Mini-Lab 4.4.

Mini-Lab 4.4: Design and Procedure Elements

Even though the design and procedure elements appear at the end of the method section, they are instrumental to the overall structure of your AR project. Below is a list of questions to help you focus on these essential elements. Your response to these questions will also help you identify which general research method is most appropriate for your AR project.

1. What key words or phrases do you use to describe your AR project to your friends and colleagues?
2. What kinds of measures are you using and when will you administer them?
3. What analytic procedures do you plan to use on your data?

Design

Traditional educational research is divided into two general methodologies: quantitative and qualitative (Creswell, 2008). There are virtually limitless ways to categorize and characterize these two research methods. However, Mertler and Charles (2008) provide a simple metric to understand the essential difference between the two: "research that relies on narrative data is called qualitative research, while research that relies on numerical data is called quantitative research" (p. 26). Quantitative and qualitative research methods encompass an array of specific designs that will be covered in subsequent pages. For now, consider which general research method is most appropriate for your AR project by consulting Table 4.2.

First and foremost, the general research method and specific design should align with your research topic and questions. Choosing a design based entirely on familiarity (i.e., I know how to run those tests) or ease of use (i.e., I think I can do that) is not the proper point of departure. Rather, the methods you choose should be those that are most effective and appropriate for your questions of interest.

Table 4.2
Basic Elements of Research Design

	Quantitative	Qualitative
Research topic, purpose, and questions	Explanatory, focused on description of specific variables	Exploratory, open to multiple variables and phenomena
Available literature	Large and broad literature base for central questions of interest that limit and justify your research	Small and limited literature base for questions of interest that contextualize your research
Data collection	Easily measurable with traditional instruments, focused on numeric data	Difficult to measure with traditional instruments, focused on narrative data
Data analysis	Statistical analysis involving both descriptive and inferential analysis	Coding textual data to identify major themes present in the data

Note. Adapted from Creswell, 2008; Mertler, 2009.

Choosing a quantitative or qualitative research method is just the first step in articulating the specific design of your AR project. Both quantitative and qualitative methods include several specific research designs, each with its associated conditions and caveats. The following sections provide an overview of common quantitative and qualitative research designs.

Common Quantitative Research Designs

Experimental and Quasi-Experimental

Experimental research designs seek to identify and disentangle the cause and effect relationship between variables of interest. You can think of experimental research as the traditional laboratory-based inquiry where scientists attempt to demonstrate that X causes Y. In other words, experimental research designs typically manipulate some independent variable, like exposure to sunlight or participation in a novel math program, to determine the impact or outcome as measured through some dependent variable, like amount of new growth or standardized math test scores.

True experimental designs require random assignment of participants to either a treatment or control condition, careful implementation of the treatment, and precise measurement of outcome measures of interest.

True experimental research designs are relatively uncommon in AR projects. Seldom do practitioner researchers have the ability to randomly assign participants to a treatment or control condition within a given classroom or school. Therefore, when researchers encounter preexisting groups (e.g., classrooms within a school or groups of students within a classroom) they may use a quasi-experimental design. A quasi-experimental design involves "assignment, but not random assignment" (Creswell, 2008, p. 313). For example, an action researcher interested in studying the impact of an innovative math program on student math scores might assign one classroom to the new math program while the other classroom receives the traditional math curriculum. In this example, individual students are effectively assigned to an experimental or control condition based on their current classroom assignment. So, while students are assigned to a treatment or control condition, they do not have an equal and random chance of being assigned to either condition because of their preexisting placement in a given classroom. Think of a quasi-experimental design as an applied educational research method for determining if *X* causes *Y*.

When action researchers implement a quasi-experimental design, they often have an idea or hypothesis about the expected outcomes of their research project (Creswell, 2008; Mertler, 2009). A research hypothesis flows from the general research questions and is based on evidence from the research literature and personal experience. For example, if you are the math teacher implementing the math project described above, your research hypothesis may read something like this: "Students who participate in the new math program will demonstrate an increase in math test scores compared to students who do not participate in the new math program." We can presume here that the action researcher has good reason to believe the new math program will increase student math ability as measured on some test of math skills, that these reasons are based on evidence in the literature and personal experience with math instruction, and that this hypothesis is directly connected to the purpose and research questions of this AR project.

Once the research hypothesis is established, action researchers will use hypothesis testing—a common statistical procedure—to determine if their hypothesis is accurate and supported by the data. The logic and construction of hypothesis testing derives from theories of scientific knowledge (see Levinson, 1982; Shadish, Cook, & Campbell, 2002) and is built on the Aristotelian concept of *modus tollens*: if X then Y, if not X then not Y. Simply put, researchers set up a hypothesis (the null) that they attempt to disprove or reject so that the logical complement (alternative) can be accepted.

So how do researchers go about setting up hypothesis testing? Well, before any statistical analysis can be conducted you must articulate a null and alternative hypothesis. A typical null hypothesis states, "There is no relationship between independent and dependent variables or no difference between groups" (Creswell, 2008, p. 137). The alternative hypothesis, which is the logical complement of the null, asserts that there is a difference between variables or groups of interest in the study. Alternative hypotheses can be non-directional (i.e., simply that there is a difference between variables or groups) or directional (i.e., that there is a difference between groups and the researcher has evidence to support the positive or negative direction of that change). Consider the following examples of null and alternative hypotheses:

Null Hypothesis (often indicated with the symbol H_0):
There is no difference in math scores between students in the experimental (new math) and control (traditional math) groups.

Alternative Hypothesis (often indicated with the symbol H_1):
Non-directional
There is a difference in math scores between students in the experimental (new math) and control (traditional math) groups.
Directional
Students in the experimental (new math) group will demonstrate higher math scores than students in the control (traditional math) group.

Once you have articulated null and alternative hypotheses, consider how you will set up your research project to get the data you need to conduct your hypothesis test. One consideration here is whether your quasi-experimental design is within- or between-group subjects. Within-group designs measure change in a single group over a period of time (e.g., changes in math scores from quarter 1 to quarter 2 for one elementary school class). Participants in within-group designs are not compared to another group; they become their own control or comparison group. Between-group designs measure change between two or more groups (e.g., changes in math scores over the course of an academic year for an experimental and control elementary school classroom). In between-group designs, groups are compared against each other to determine the impact of some intervention or treatment.

In order to have sufficient data to make these comparisons, researchers must implement some kind of measurement tool for each participant (this is true for both within- and between-group designs). The most common approach to data collection for quasi-experimental designs is the pre- and posttest method. The terms pretest and posttest refer to the time at which the measurement instrument is implemented in the experimental design. Said another way, pretests are administered before the intervention and treatment, and posttests are administered when the intervention or treatment is complete. The pre- and posttest method of data collection is an essential design element that, when implemented effectively, book-ends or encapsulates the intervention or treatment and provides important information about change within the intervention window.

Creswell (2008) provides three succinct requirements for implementing an effective quasi-experimental design (p. 305).

1. Identify a treatment variable
   Example: Type of mathematics instruction in elementary classroom
2. Identify the conditions (or levels) of the variable
   Example: Traditional math curriculum
   Example: Traditional math curriculum with additional activities
3. Manipulate the treatment conditions
   Example: Provide manipulatives and additional supplemental activities to the "treatment" condition

Correlational

Correlational designs examine "whether and to what degree a statistical relationship exists between two or more variables" (Mertler, 2009, p. 83). Another way to think about a correlation is the degree to which two variables co-vary or change together. This change can be positive (i.e., when one variable increases, so does the other variable) or negative (i.e., when one variable increases, the other decreases). The specific indicators of the direction and strength of these relationships will be discussed in the findings chapter. For now, it is important to remember that correlational designs describe the general relationship between variables of interest.

Unlike a quasi-experimental design, correlational designs do not require random assignment or the manipulation of a treatment condition. In fact, correlations are typically conducted on existing data for only one group of participants. For example, an action researcher might be interested to know if there is a correlation between the time spent on homework and test grades in a particular math class. The researcher could ask students to estimate the total time dedicated to studying math in a given week, and then collect existing math test scores from those students. This correlational design and subsequent data collection would support an analysis that examined the movement of one variable (math test scores) with the movement of the other (time spent studying).

Because correlational designs do not require random assignment or the implementation of an intervention or treatment, they do not support causal claims. Said another way, no matter how strong the relationship, a correlation does not imply causation. It is easy to slip into causal claims unless you are diligent in your interpretation of the data and write-up of the results. Think about the example above. It is quite possible that there is a high, positive correlation between time studying and math test scores. And you may even be tempted to assert that an increase in study time causes an increase in math test scores. While this interpretation may seem plausible, it is not supported by the kind of research design described here. Remember, correlational designs simply describe "relationships between two or more variables" (Mertler & Charles, 2008, p. 248).

Consider the following basic components of a correlational design:

1. Identify the variables of interest
   Example: Time spent studying math in a given week; Scores on chapter math tests
2. Identify participants and collect data for each variable
   Example: Access chapter test scores for all students in your math class; Ask students to report the amount of time they spend studying math in a given week

Survey

Survey designs cover a broad array of research methods ranging from Internet surveys to individual interviews. As we discussed in the previous section, survey designs are a common method for assessing general characteristics of a given population. For this reason, Mertler and Charles (2008) state, "survey research is also sometimes referred to as descriptive research" (p. 225). A properly constructed survey design will allow for comparative and correlational analysis in addition to the traditional descriptive research.

When researchers talk about survey design they are commonly referring to the conditions and requirements for creating a survey instrument. Survey design as a research methodology includes those elements specific to instrument design and much more. Perhaps the most important consideration in survey design methodology is the type of survey being implemented. Most social scientists identify three major types of surveys: descriptive, cross-sectional, and longitudinal (Creswell, 2008; Mertens, 1998; Mertler & Charles, 2008).

Descriptive surveys are often described as "one-shot" opportunities to describe some salient feature or characteristic of a population of interest. As such, descriptive surveys give detailed information about a group of people (e.g., elementary school students) at a specific point in time. Cross-sectional surveys are an extension of the descriptive survey in that they examine salient features or characteristics of multiple groups at the same time. For example, a cross-sectional survey could be used in the hypothetical research scenario regarding Saint Michael School to assess parent, teacher, and parishioner perceptions of the proposed school consolidation. The benefit of including multiple groups is that you could analyze responses to survey questions based on certain demographic information (e.g., stakeholder group, years affiliated with the school, etc.).

Finally, the longitudinal survey design extends the basic descriptive method by including the element of time. Longitudinal surveys typically assess the same participants over a given period of time (i.e., weeks, months, years). This design allows researchers to identify the development of certain characteristics or measure changes in perceptions and practices within a given sample. Longitudinal survey designs can be difficult to maintain since the researcher must be able to contact participants over an extended period of time—during which participants may graduate from school, move to a new city, change occupations, and so on.

Creswell (2008) notes that cross-sectional survey designs are the most commonly used method in survey research. However, there are benefits and drawbacks to each. Consider the following basic components of survey design:

1. Identify variables of interest
   Example: Perceptions of proposed school consolidation
2. Identify participants
   Example: Parents, teachers, and parishioners
3. Identify timeframe and administer survey
   Example: Administer survey to key stakeholders after Thanksgiving break

Common Qualitative Designs

Grounded Theory

Strauss and Corbin (1998) define grounded theory as "theory that was derived from data, systematically gathered and analyzed through the research process" (p. 12). Rather than testing a theory or specific hypothesis, grounded theory design systematically utilizes qualitative methods of data collection and analysis to build theory. As such, a grounded theory design is ideal for analyzing processes in a small group (e.g., classroom) or organization (e.g., school).

Grounded theory designs typically rely on qualitative methods such as interviews, observations, and researcher notes or commentary to generate data for theory building. Once the data are collected, researchers must sift and sort through voluminous textual evidence to identify and define major themes. Although there is some debate regarding the specific structure and flexibility of grounded theory research, social scientists generally agree that grounded theory offers a "step-by-step, systematic procedure" for analyzing data (Creswell, 2008, p. 432).

The first type of grounded theory design is called "the systematic design." This design is so named because of the reliance on a systematic movement through prescribed procedural elements. These procedural elements shape the analysis of the data and include open coding, axial coding, and selective coding (Creswell, 2008; Strauss & Corbin, 1998). Open coding is the first pass through the data wherein researchers identify major categories. In the second step, axial coding, the researcher places each open code "at the center of the process being explored (as the core phenomenon) and then relates other categories to it" (Creswell, 2008, p. 434). At this stage of coding, a diagram of the open and axial codes is developed to demonstrate the connection or relationship among variables. Finally, in selective coding, the researcher begins to articulate a theory to describe the relationship of all axial codes that have been developed.

The final two types of grounded theory research—emerging and constructivist designs—were developed in response to the highly structured and ordered procedure of the systematic grounded theory design. As such, both the emerging and constructivist designs are more flexible and fluid forms of grounded theory research. The focus of the emerging design is on "connecting categories" (Creswell, 2008, p. 438). Themes and theories emerge from these connected categories and are not reliant on structured, a priori categories (i.e., axial codes). Constructivist grounded theory design is a balance between the systematic and emerging designs that focuses on the values and feelings of the participants. For example, a constructivist approach to grounded theory is as much interested in participants' perception of and feelings about a particular event as a rich description of the event itself. Constructivists are concerned with what a phenomenon "is" and what it "means" for the people in a particular community.

Consider the following basic components of grounded theory design:

1. Identify a "process, action, or interaction to study" (Creswell, 2008, p. 432)
   Example: How first generation immigrant children develop English language competency in my school
2. Engage key stakeholders
   Example: Conduct interviews and focus groups with first generation immigrant children in my school, their parents, and the teachers responsible for helping them to learn English

Case Study

A case study is "an in-depth exploration of a bounded system (e.g., an activity, event, process, or individuals) based on extensive data collection" (Creswell, 2008, p. 476). Unlike grounded theory designs that are meant to produce theory or explanation of an entire group or process, the purpose of a case study is to "develop a highly detailed description and gain an understanding of the individual entity" (Mertler & Charles, 2008, p. 196). The "case" in case study designs can be a single person, a small group, a classroom, or school. The cases could also be the focus of a grounded theory design, yet there is an important distinction to remember: case study designs focus on rich, detailed description of the individual case whereas grounded theory designs focus on describing the processes in order to develop overarching theories.

There are three primary types of case studies that serve complementary purposes in this qualitative research design: intrinsic, instrumental, and collective (Creswell, 2008). Intrinsic cases are those that are unique, unusual, or different than the norm. For example, a dual-language immersion school that enrolls 50% native English speaking and 50% native Spanish speaking students would be an intrinsic case in the study of English language acquisition of first generation immigrant children. Instrumental cases highlight important features of an educational issue. For example, the hypothetical research scenario involving Saint Michael School is an instrumental case as it provides a prototypical example of issues facing many urban Catholic schools in the United States. Finally, a collective case, as the name implies, is a comparison across several individual cases that highlights important features of a specific educational issue. For example, in a collective case study, you may conduct cross-case comparisons of several Catholic schools that effectively engage and serve Latino children in their community. This process would illuminate key similarities and differences across cases, and provide a fuller understanding of Latino enrollment in Catholic schools. Consider the following basic components of case study design:

1. Identify the "case"
   Example: A Catholic school that successfully engages and serves Latino children and families in their community
2. Engage key stakeholders
   Example: Pastor, principal, teachers, parents

It should be noted here that, although case study designs are generally considered qualitative research, many case studies often use some combination of quantitative and qualitative methods. In fact, most AR projects will include both quantitative and qualitative elements.

Mixed Methods Design

Although educational research methods are traditionally characterized as either quantitative or qualitative, many applied educational research projects adopt a mixed method design—a combination of both quantitative and qualitative methods. There are several types of mixed methods designs that rely, in varying degrees, on the methods, data, and analytic procedures of quantitative and qualitative methods. For example, you may use quantitative and qualitative methods simultaneously and in tandem to address your questions of interest (triangulation). Alternatively, you might begin your study with a quantitative analysis and then follow up with qualitative methods to explain the nature of the relationships identified (explanatory), or you may use qualitative data to frame your research and rely on quantitative methods to explore the nature of those relationships (exploratory; see Creswell, 2008, pp. 556-562).

You may find that none of the mixed method designs described above fit your research project exactly. That is perfectly fine. The methods you use for your own AR project should be specific to your research questions and context, and may not fit neatly into one of these categories or molds. In fact, you may find varying degrees of priority between quantitative and qualitative methods depending on the phase or stage of your research. Ultimately, your topic and specific research questions will determine the appropriate "mix" of quantitative and qualitative methods in your AR project. Consider what quantitative and qualitative elements you will include in your AR project in Mini-Lab 4.5.

Mini-Lab 4.5: Deciding on Your Design

Describe to a friend or colleague what your research project "looks like." As you describe your AR project, consider the following questions. When you are finished, write down what method or combination of methods best meets the objectives of your AR project.

1. What are the major research questions you hope to answer?
2. How will you collect data? Who will be participating in your AR project?
3. Will you be focusing on numeric or textual data?
4. What is your general timeline?

Common Research Designs and Analytic Procedures

Analytic procedures are an important component of your research design and overall AR project. Analytic procedures determine how you will use the data to respond to your questions of interest. How can you identify general trends in the data? What differences exist between groups or over time? Is there a relationship between your variables of interest? What are the central themes that emerge from your interview data? To answer these questions you must choose and implement the appropriate analytic procedure. Detailed instructions for conducting these analyses are included in the following chapter. For now, consider which of these analytic procedures (see Table 4.3) seems most appropriate for your AR project, design, and data.

Table 4.3
General Analytic Procedures

Analysis	General description	Common design
Descriptive	Provides information about specific responses (e.g., mean score for survey items) and general trends or patterns in the data	Quasi-Experimental Correlational Survey Grounded Theory Case Study
t test	Determines the significance of the difference between two means	Quasi-Experimental Survey
ANOVA	Determines the significance of the difference between two or more means	Quasi-Experimental Survey
Correlation	Determines the strength and direction of the relationship between two or more variables of interest	Correlational Survey
Coding	Organizes textual data into categories and major themes; highlights salient connections among themes	Grounded Theory Case Study

Procedure

In addition to the major design elements of your AR project, the method section must also contain a general timeline of the major events and activities of your research. It is important to let the reader know when you began your research, when your surveys or interviews were administered, when and for how long your innovative math curriculum was being used, and so on. Month and year are sufficient to convey the general timeline of your major components (e.g., surveys were administered in September 2009). Although procedural elements are a separate and distinct requirement within the method section, you may find that they fit best nestled within the description of your design elements when you are writing your final report. Researchers often discuss essential design components and procedural elements together to provide a concise description of the segments and sequencing of the research project (see Mini-Lab 4.6).

Mini-Lab 4.6: Procedural Timeline

Providing information on the sequence of events is an important component of your action research paper. A well-articulated timeline organizes the major elements of your research into clearly identifiable segments. On a separate sheet of paper, create a timeline of all major research activities in your AR project. Start from the very beginning of the school year through to the conclusion of your AR project.

Figure 4.10   Outline for Constructing the Method Section

Method
1. Method Introduction
    a. Brief review of the purpose and context of your action research project.
    b. General overview of procedures and protocol.
2. Participants
    a. Description of the people who participated in the study.
        i. Example: students, faculty, parents, school administrators, etc.
    b. If more than one group participated, provide relevant overall information (all groups together) in addition to the group-specific information.
    c. Total number of participants, age (average and range where appropriate), gender, religious identity, ethnicity, and any other relevant information.
    d. Description of the context or environment where the study was conducted.
        i. Example: third grade classroom at a K-8 Catholic school, rural regional parish school, monthly faculty meetings in school library, etc.
3. Instruments/Materials
    a. Description of the materials or programs used in the study.
        i. Example: after school reading program, revised math curriculum, professional development series for faculty, etc.
        ii. Samples of these materials may be included in an appendix
    b. Description of all assessment instruments used in the study.
        i. Example: standardized tests, survey instruments, interview protocol, observations, etc.
        ii. Samples of these materials may be included in an appendix
4. Design and Procedure
    a. Description of the length of the study in terms of days, months, or academic calendar markers such as quarters or semesters.
    b. Description of data collection procedures. When were the data collected, under what conditions, in what context, and how many times?
    c. Description of how you have organized and analyzed your data.
        i. Example: (Quantitative) This study used a between subject, pre- and posttest design. Participants in the control condition ($n = 185$) received traditional instruction, while participants in the experimental condition ($n = 185$) received differentiated instruction. A gain score t test was conducted to determine the effect of differentiated instruction on reading comprehension.
        ii. Example: (Qualitative) This study used an ethnographic design to examine community members' beliefs and attitudes regarding the consolidation of several Catholic schools in an urban, Midwestern city. Interview and focus group responses with teachers, parents, and students were transcribed and text segments were coded. Codes were reduced and collapsed into seven major themes.
5. Educational research papers do not typically include general summary or integration commentary at the end of the method section.

Summary Guidelines for Method

The method section is a blueprint or guide for the design, content, and process of your AR project. Figure 4.10 is a template to use as a general guide when constructing your method section.

Conclusion

The paradox of the method section is that you are required to provide massive amounts of technical and procedural information through succinct, compact, and scientific writing. You, like many action researchers before you, might find the writing in this section to be abrupt or terse, disjointed by multiple sub-sections, and unlike any other writing you have done before. That is perfectly acceptable. Remember, the point of the method section is to describe the essential elements of your AR project and the connection between your research questions and research design without being overly narrative or verbose.

Action Research in Action:
Method Section

Method

The purpose of this action research project was to explore stakeholder perceptions of the proposed school consolidation plan. An original survey instrument and semi-structured interviews were used in this mixed-method study.

Participants

Participants ($N = 94$) were 30 parishioner-parents of current students (10 male, 20 female), 27 non-parishioner-parents of current students (9 male, 18 female), 25 parishioners without school-age children (9 male, 16 female), and 12 teachers (3 male, 9 female). Participants had between 3 and 30 years of affiliation with the parish or school ($M = 16.7$ years affiliation; $SD = 6.1$). All participants were selected from a convenience sample of individuals who responded to an announcement in the parish bulletin and school newsletter.

Instruments and Materials

Survey instrument. An original survey instrument was used to assess stakeholder perceptions of access to an education at Saint Michael School and general thoughts on the proposed school consolidation (see Appendix A). The survey instrument consisted of five statements and a corresponding 4-point Likert scale ranging from *Strongly Agree* (1) to *Strongly Disagree* (4). Participants were asked to indicate their level of agreement or disagreement with questions such as "The proposed school consolidation will be beneficial for Saint Michael Parish."

Interview protocol. An original interview protocol was used in this study to engage stakeholders at Saint Michael Parish and School in questions regarding the impact of consolidation on their community (see Appendix B). The semi-structured interview protocol consisted of five open-ended questions that addressed affiliation with the school and perception of the consolidation. Participants were asked to respond to questions such as "What is your biggest concern regarding the proposed consolidation?"

Design and Procedure

      This mixed-method action research project employed a cross-sectional survey and semi-structured interview to address the primary questions of interest. All participants ($N =$ 94) completed the survey instrument, and a sub-sample ($n = 10$) completed the semi-structured interview. Multiple data points (i.e., surveys and interviews) with community stakeholders (i.e., parents, teachers, and parishioners) were used to triangulate and validate the data.

      An announcement explaining this action research project appeared in the parish bulletin and school newsletter in September 2010, two weeks after a series of town hall meetings to discuss the proposed consolidation of several local Catholic schools. Interested participants provided their contact information and were mailed a consent form (see Appendix C) and a paper survey to complete at their convenience. Completed surveys and consent forms were returned to the researcher in a self-addressed, stamped envelope. The same sample of participants was contacted independent of the request to complete the survey to participate in an individual interview with the researcher. Interviews were conducted at Saint Michael School in the researcher's office. Interviews were audio recorded and typically lasted between 30 to 45 minutes. Survey and interview data collection was completed by December 2010.

      In addition to the survey and interview data, the researcher collected school enrollment data for the past 5 years. This data was used to establish a general trajectory of enrollment trends at Saint Michael School and to address concerns about declining enrollment that were expressed in the survey and interviews.

Findings

      The purpose of this action research project was to examine factors that impact the accessibility and affordability of a Saint Michael education, and explore stakeholder perceptions of the proposed consolidation plan. An original survey instrument and semi-structured interviews were used in this mixed-method study. An analysis of variance (ANOVA) was used to analyze

5

Findings

In the findings section, believe it or not, there is a story to be told and you must be the storyteller. Now that you have executed your research methods and your data have been collected, consider for a moment the notion offered by Sagor (2005): There is a story laying dormant and trapped inside and among your data; your job as a data analyst is to liberate that story "and give it an opportunity to take form and reveal itself" (p. 109). The findings section of your research paper is where you do just that. Here you present the outcomes of your quantitative and/or qualitative analyses. The *Publication Manual of the American Psychological Association* states that this section should "summarize the collected data and the analysis performed on those data relevant to the discourse that is to follow" (APA, 2010, p. 32). This section is critical to the validity of your study and the generalizability of your conclusions.

The findings section takes you back to the very questions that prompted your action research in the first place. Robinson and Lai (2006) explain that at this stage, all of your data—from interviews, surveys, focus groups, assessments, observations— are used to "propose answers to your research questions" (p. 141). Even more directly, they state: "The goal of the data analysis phase is to provide valid answers to your research questions" (p. 141). Your charge as you proceed through the data analysis process is to distill "vast amounts of data into smaller, more manageable sets of information" (Mertler, 2009, p. 139).

As evidenced via the following viewpoints, there is a true satisfaction in now being positioned to answer the questions that you proposed at the outset; concurrently, though, it is easy to feel overwhelmed, awash in numbers and text. For example, Robinson and Lai (2006) contend that "the process of analyzing information gathered through interviews, observations, and fieldwork is the most exciting part of doing research" (p. 141). As a counterpoint, Mertler (2009) observes that this is "probably the step during which inexperienced researchers encounter the most anxiety" (p. 139). It is likely that both of these sentiments will ring true for you, since it can be challenging and energizing work "to identify the aspects of the information that will assist people in…providing accounts of *what* is happening and *how* it is happening" (Stringer, 2007, p. 95).

We echo the sentiment that "findings and conclusions do not materialize out of thin air—they come from careful scrutiny of your data as you proceed through a systematic process of making sense of what you learned" (Dana & Yendol-Silva, 2003, p. 89). Analytic results should be presented in a clear and concise manner with sufficient detail. You must display and present your evidence. Extensive commentary on the results is not warranted in this section; expository writing is the function of the discussion section. It is important to also include results that run counter to your predictions or confound your questions of interest. This chapter will describe the processes for preparing your data for analysis, the common analytical procedures that you may use, how best to present your findings, and how to ensure the validity of your action research.

Preparing Your Data

People sometimes chuckle at first hearing the suggestion that they need to "clean their data." One might ask, "What's wrong with my data? Why are they unclean?" Researchers often use the term raw data to refer to data that are directly from sources and are unprocessed, unanalyzed, unedited, and unchecked. Examples include a recording of an interview with the associate pastor on a digital voice recorder, a stack of hand-written surveys that you collected from the preschool staff, a set of journal entries from the new theology teacher, or a data spreadsheet of your parishioner survey that you have downloaded from SurveyMonkey. To ensure the highest possible accuracy and credibility of your data analysis, you must invest some time at the front end to make sure that your data are reviewed, checked, and organized prior to analysis. Correctly preparing your quantitative and qualitative data will ensure that your analyses are accurate and will save you time in the long run. Guidance is provided for preparing both qualitative and quantitative data.

Preparation of Qualitative Data

For qualitative research approaches, Hendricks (2006) notes that the first step is converting all collected data to textual form. McLellan, MacQueen, and Neidig (2003) offer excellent guidance on the preparation and organization of textual data. They suggest that:

- Transcriptions of interviews, focus groups, and so on, should all be similarly formatted, using the same type of font, spacing, and text justifications.

- All transcripts should be completely labeled at the top with information such as participant name or ID, interview/focus group date, time, location, and interviewer or facilitator name.
- Verbatim transcriptions (i.e., exactly as recorded, word for word) are preferred, including mispronounced words, slang, grammatical errors, and filler words (e.g., um, ah, uh huh).

To audit your completed transcription for accuracy, "the transcriber/proofreader shall check (proofread) all transcriptions against the audiotape and revise the transcript file accordingly" (McLellan et al., 2003, p. 80). If your qualitative data are in the form of journals or documents, no transcription is necessary, although at this stage all materials should be labeled, catalogued, and collated in one place.

Consult Appendix A to review an example of a qualitative interview data set based on the Saint Michael School Consolidation study. The appendix contains a subset of interview transcripts derived from the face-to-face, semi-structured interviews that Mrs. Theresa Q. Principal conducted with teachers, parishioner-parents, and non-parishioner parents. In accordance with the procedures for preparing qualitative data outlined above, note that each transcript features uniform formatting, a descriptive labeling system, and a verbatim transcription.

Preparation of Quantitative Data

Before running any analyses on your quantitative data, you want to be sure that you have checked, reviewed, and organized your data. Let us consider the Saint Michael Parish and School Survey as an example. All five questions on the survey provide a response set with four options that range from *Strongly Disagree* to *Strongly Agree*. In this case, and in many others, a standard practice is to organize your data spreadsheet so that respondent number (or participant ID or some other identifier) is listed down the far left column and across the top of the spreadsheet each column is labeled to represent one of the five items on the survey. Imagine that you now have the stack of completed surveys from the 12 teachers at Saint Michael School and you are ready to enter their responses into an Excel spreadsheet.

First, you need a strategy, or coding scheme, to translate their word responses (e.g., *disagree*) into number responses. A typical conversion format would be to code responses so that *Strongly Disagree* = 1, *Disagree* = 2, *Agree* = 3 and *Strongly Agree* = 4. A good rule of thumb when recoding from verbal response categories to numeric values is that higher amounts or levels of the construct in question (in this case, level of agreement) should correspond to higher numeric values. Striving for that type of alignment allows for a more intuitive discussion of what the values mean. On a student effort survey designed by Kmack (2008), for example, higher values correspond to more effort expended in the student advisory program.

Second, once your data are entered, you must check for data entry errors like out-of-range values and possible outliers. When keying in data from an original survey source, it is possible, especially with large datasets, that human error contributes to typographical errors in entering values: a 4 is entered as 44 or a letter is inserted instead of a number. Thus, you must check each column of data for values that are outside the range of accepted values for the item in question. For the first item on the School Perception Survey, based on the coding scheme described above, only four possible values are valid entries: 1, 2, 3, and 4. When you review that column of data, you immediately know there is an error if any other values are present.

Another data error to be cognizant of are outliers. Data analysts identifying outliers in large datasets sometimes use complex formulas to detect values that are "far" from the mean, using the standard deviation as a metric to judge distance from the mean. Within the relatively smaller datasets that action researchers typically encounter, outliers can be detected by using Excel to sort a particular variable, from lowest to highest values. Simply examining values at the high and low ends of the distribution of scores often indicates an outlier. For example, suppose you have asked teachers to indicate their years of experience serving in Catholic schools. When you sort the data according to that variable, you note that a few teachers have reported "1" at the low end of the distribution—certainly a plausible and not unlikely pattern. However, at the upper end of the distribution, you note the following values: 107 and 66. The first is impossible for the question you have posed, and even the second is questionable. In this case, it would be wise to remove the 107 value from the dataset and to re-check the other value; it may be that 66 was inadvertently entered for 6.

Figure 5.1   Preparing Quantitative Data for Analysis in Excel

Organizing Data for t Test and Correlation Analysis

Participant ID	Variable 1 (e.g., pretest score)	Variable 2 (e.g., posttest score)
1	XX	YY
2	XX	YY
3	XX	YY
4	XX	YY

Organizing Data for ANOVA

Principal Responses	Teacher Responses	Parent Responses
XX	YY	ZZ
XX	YY	ZZ
XX	YY	ZZ
XX	YY	ZZ

Third, quantitative data can require some reconfiguration before it is in a form that is recognizable by even the most basic software programs. There are certain default ways in which common programs "read" your data; setting up your data in a manner that is congruent with these default settings will also save time and energy in the long run. If Excel is the primary platform for data analysis, it is helpful to set up your data in adjacent columns for items that will be compared via a *t* test or correlation analysis, and separate data into group columns for ANOVA (see Figure 5.1).

Mini-Lab 5.1: Preparing Your Data for Analysis

To prepare your data for analysis, make sure that you carefully review your raw data prior to conducting any analyses or calculations.

1. For your qualitative data, have you
    a. Converted all data to textual form? _____
    b. Utilized verbatim transcription? _____
    c. Formatted transcripts similarly? _____
    d. Created a detailed label for each transcript? _____
    e. Rechecked the transcript against the audiotape? _____

2. For your quantitative data, have you
    a. Developed a workable spreadsheet format? _____
    b. Converted all word responses into number responses (e.g., *always* = 1, *sometimes* = 2, etc.)? _____
    c. Identified potential outliers and/or mis-keyed data? _____
    d. Arranged your spreadsheet data so that data analyses can be conducted efficiently (e.g., arranging variables side-by-side for correlation and *t* test; arranging groups side-by-side for ANOVA)? _____

Common Analytical Procedures for Qualitative Data

This section provides an overview of common analytic procedures and provides examples based on the Saint Michael research scenario. While this is not an exhaustive list of analysis approaches, these are the most commonly employed in our research courses. For more advanced analyses, or for more information on these analyses, see our list of resources.

Qualitative Analysis

The process of qualitative analysis is an inductive, iterative analysis approach that ultimately seeks to make meaning from your multiple data sources. "Inductive analysis means to look at a field or group of data and try to induce or create order by organizing what is observed into groups" (Johnson, 2008, p. 103). As described earlier, by this point your data sources have been converted into textual form and the task at hand is to fully engage with those texts through a process of reading and distilling, always attentive to emerging patterns and themes. As the source texts are read and re-read, often several times, qualitative action researchers attempt to discern ordered patterns that seem to cut across the data. Several methodologists have articulated strategies for conducting these qualitative analyses in ways that are rigorous, replicable, accurate, and trustworthy (Creswell, 2006; Strauss & Corbin, 1998). Generally speaking, these strategies use a process of coding to isolate, extract, and describe the most meaningful overarching themes from your textual data.

One straightforward approach to coding a qualitative dataset is outlined here. The first key step is to familiarize yourself with the dataset, best achieved through multiple readings of the data. Second, you begin the process of open coding. In open coding, you make an initial attempt to bring forth the major emerging categories within the data. As the name implies, at this stage the coding is preliminary, exploratory, evolving, and open to revision. A goal of this step is to highlight and bring to the surface some of the abstract concepts that rest deep within the data. For example, suppose you are analyzing the data from the transcribed, semi-structured interviews with Saint Michael parishioners, focusing on the item, "What is your biggest concern regarding the proposed consolidation?" After previewing and familiarizing yourself with the responses, you might use a graphic organizer like Table 5.1 to compile your open coding results. The second and third interviews contained in Appendix A provide a visual example of an interview transcript containing first-level qualitative coding. Pertinent text segments are color coded to represent distinct abstract concepts that have emerged from the interview dialogue.

Table 5.1
Coding Qualitative Data

Preliminary name of code	Number of references
Loss of parish-school connection	45
Losing historical connection	41
Consolidation is a viable strategy	30
Direct resistance to consolidation	25
Action researcher creates exhaustive list of open codes here.....	

It is good practice to be self-reflexive at this point, challenging yourself to consider why you selected the codes that you did. Be aware of how your own experience, bias, position, or opinion on the issue might have factored into your open coding process. Review and revise as necessary.

The third step seeks greater convergence among the data as you try to observe where there are points of overlap among the open codes. Where such overlap is detected, can a consolidated—albeit slightly more expansive—code be generated? In reviewing the open codes in Table 5.1, some similarity is apparent between "Loss of parish-school connection" and "Losing historical connection." Upon reviewing all of the text references that correspond to those two codes, you might make the determination that it is appropriate to create a new collapsed code. The participants' responses seem to indicate that in many ways the current identity is shaped by the parish's history and tradition. Therefore, you create a new collapsed code named "Loss of parish-school connection—Historical and current." In many qualitative action research projects, the initial open coding list can be quite extensive, so the process of refining, combining, and collapsing codes is essential. To complete this step, continue to combine all overlapping and related codes as needed to develop a final list of collapsed codes. As before, be especially reflective about how and why you are organizing the codes as you are. It is helpful to create a codebook that summarizes your coding process, containing a tabular presentation of each code, a description, and a representative quote or two.

Fourth, with your data now aligned into a system of categories—your collapsed codes—you should be able to discern major themes. Start by selecting the most important, interesting, or robust categories, and then review the data related to those categories again. What themes can you draw from the data? What claims might you be able to make based on these data? Only make claims that you feel are supported by the data you have available. You might also find that the themes you arrive at tend to vary across stakeholder groups. Thus, returning to our example, you might note that while "Direct resistance to consolidation" was a primary theme among the open-ended responses, that sentiment was markedly more pronounced among one stakeholder group, parishioners/parents of current Saint Michael's students.

While there are qualitative data analysis software programs that can assist with this process (NVivo, Ethnograph, among others), they are not necessary. These types of analyses can be conducted with low-tech tools such as a series of colored highlighters, each color used to mark a particular code (see Appendix A). A standard word processing program also offers a functional approach in which text segments can be highlighted, color-coded, and even appended with comments/notes via an editing tool like "Track Changes" in Microsoft Word. Users more comfortable with Excel have used its spreadsheet capabilities and management of multiple data sheets to sort, sift, and organize qualitative data. Whichever method you choose, the goal remains the same: systematically sorting and re-organizing textual data to arrive at the major conceptual underpinnings and conclusions that lend meaning to the data.

Common Analytical Procedures for Quantitative Data

Statistics Dashboard

We could write an entire book on the common analytic procedures for quantitative data—indeed many social scientists have done just that. However, our goal here is to provide a broad and basic overview of the analytic procedures so that you are comfortable with their design and requirements, and can make appropriate decisions about your own AR project. To facilitate this process we have designed a *Statistics Dashboard* (see Mini-Lab 5.2 and Figure 5.2) as a guide for quantitative analysis. This document will provide the basic framework for all major quantitative analyses.

Mini-Lab 5.2: Get Behind the Wheel and Use the Statistics Dashboard

The logic of hypothesis testing can seem confusing at first, but the Statistics Dashboard (see Figure 5.2) takes a stepwise approach to the matter. If you are conducting quantitative analyses as part of your AR project, take a moment now to think through your analytic procedure. Complete Part I (Preparing for the Inferential Test) and Part II (Conducting the Test and Making a Conclusion) of the Statistics Dashboard.

Figure 5.2   Statistics Dashboard

Part I – Preparing for the Inferential Test			
1	State the Null Hypothesis:	**2**	State the Alternative Hypothesis:
3	Select the Level of Significance—Alpha Level—for Rejecting the Null Hypothesis: Less Conservative .05 .01 More Conservative .001	**4**	Select Your Test: t test: Comparing two groups ANOVA: Comparing two or more groups Correlation: Relationship between two continuous variables Chi-Square: Comparing frequencies and proportions Regression: Using two or more variables to predict an outcome variable

Figure 5.2   Statistics Dashboard (*continued*)

Part II – Conducting the Test and Making a Conclusion			
5	Run Your Test and Report the Test Statistic (t, F, r, X^2, or *beta*): _____ = _____	6	Report the Probability Level Associated with Your Test Statistic: p = _____
7	Make a Decision about Rejecting or Failing to Reject the Null Hypothesis: Is the p-value that you obtained (item 6) greater than or less than the significance level (item 3)? If it is greater, you ACCEPT or RETAIN the Null Hypothesis (item 1). If it is less than, you REJECT the Null Hypothesis and ACCEPT the Alternative Hypothesis (item 2). Your finding is STATISTICALLY SIGNIFICANT.	8	Make a concluding statistical statement: t test: There was a significant difference between the test scores at Time 1 (M = 89.2) compared to Time 2 (M = 97.1), $t(57)$ = 3.14, $p < .05$. ANOVA: Average number of tardies per quarter differed among Grade 2, Grade 4, and Grade 8, $F(2, 134)$ = 3.12, $p < .05$. Correlation: Scores on the High School Placement Test showed a significant positive correlation with high school GPA, $r(145)$ = .67, $p < .01$. Regression: Family income (beta = .34, $p < .05$) and ethnic identity (beta = .27, $p < .05$) were both significant predictors of adolescents' acculturation level.

Descriptive Statistics

Recall that descriptive statistics help you to determine key information about your data and include measures of central tendency (e.g., mean, median, and mode) and measures of variability (e.g., range, variance, standard deviation). Excel offers a simple feature for calculating the descriptive statistics for a single variable. Thus, assuming that your data are in a single column (i.e., array) in Excel:

1. Select the Data Tab, and click Data Analysis.
2. Select Descriptive Statistics from the list and click OK.
3. In the Input Range, enter the cell addresses for your column of data (include the Label in your selection).

4. Click the Labels box so that the variable label is included.
5. Review the Output Options and indicate the cell address where you want the output.
6. Check the Summary Statistics box.
7. Click OK for your output.

It is also possible to use this Descriptive Statistics function on several columns of data at once, if desired. All procedures are the same, except that the input range will begin with the label of the first column of data and will extend to the last value in the last column of data. The output that you receive will contain the primary measures of central tendency and variability that are of interest to you: mean, median, mode, standard deviation, range, minimum, maximum, and count.

Comparing Two Groups or One Group at Two Time Points (*t* Tests)

Recall from the previous chapter that when you want to determine whether the means of two groups are different, an independent *t* test is the appropriate test statistic (between-group analysis). Another *t* test variation, the dependent or paired-samples *t* test, is appropriate for examining the same group at two different time points, comparing the group mean at Time 1 to the group mean at Time 2 to assess whether there is a significant difference (within-group analysis). A specific *t* test scenario based on the Saint Michael project would be to compare the mean scores on an item (e.g., "Saint Michael School has sufficient resources to meet the needs of its students without consolidating") between parishioners (Group 1) and non-parishioners (Group 2).

To efficiently run a *t* test in Excel, it is helpful to align the variables that will be tested into adjacent columns. Then, use the Data Analysis ToolPak in Excel to conduct the test:

1. Select the Data Tab, and click Data Analysis.
2. Select *t* test: Two-Sample Assuming Equal Variances from the list and click OK [Recall that this is what we would select for the parishioner/non-parishioner comparison. If, however, you have the same group, compared at two time points, select *t* test: Paired Two-Sample for Means].
3. In the Variable 1 Range, enter the cell addresses for the first group of data (include the Group 1 Label in your selection).
4. In the Variable 2 Range, enter the cell addresses for the second group of data (include the Group 2 Label in your selection).
5. Place a "0" in the Hypothesized Mean Difference box.
6. Click the Labels box so that the group labels are included.
7. Confirm that the alpha level is set to 0.05.
8. Click the Output Range button and enter the cell address where you want

the output located.

9. Click OK for your output.

Excel will produce an output table that contains 11 pieces of information, which are summarized in Table 5.2. The first row of the table provides the Group 1 mean and the Group 2 mean. A quick review of the means lets you see on a basic descriptive level whether there appear to be any differences or not. Beyond that rough gauge, the t test statistic and its accompanying p value allow you to discern whether a statistically significant difference exists.

Table 5.2
Guide to t Test Output

Term	Definition
Mean	Arithmetic mean or average for each variable
Variance	Calculated variance for each variable
Observations	Total observations (data points) for each variable
Pooled variance	Total or "pooled" variance for all variables
Hypothesized mean difference	What you indicated to be the expected difference
df	Degrees of freedom
t Stat	Calculated value of t statistic, referred to as test statistic
P(T<=t) one-tail	p-value for a one-tailed t test
t Critical one-tail	Critical value for one-tailed t test
P(T<=t) two-tail	p-value for a two-tailed t test
t Critical two-tail	Critical value for two-tailed t test

Comparing Two or More Groups or Comparing One Group at Two or More Time Points (Analysis of Variance or ANOVA)

Recall from the previous chapter that when you want to determine whether the means of two or more groups are different, an ANOVA is the appropriate test statistic. A variation of the ANOVA allows you to examine the same group at two or more different time points, comparing the group means at Time 1, Time 2, Time 3, and so forth to assess whether there is a significant change across testing points.

Use the Data Analysis ToolPak to conduct an Analysis of Variance:

1. Select the Data Tab, and click Data Analysis
2. Select the proper ANOVA analysis (e.g., ANOVA: Single Factor) from the list and click OK
3. Click whether the data are Grouped By: Columns or Rows (and it will almost always be grouped by columns).
4. Click the Labels box so that labels are included.

5. Click the Output Range button and enter an address where you want the output located on the same worksheet as the data.
6. Click OK for your output.

Excel provides ANOVA output that is similar to the output generated for the *t* test analysis (see Table 5.3). In addition to looking for significance (i.e., *p* value) check the other descriptive statistics such as the listing of each group, the number of observations in each group, and the mean scores to make sure that your analysis has been correctly and accurately calculated in Excel.

Table 5.3
Guide to ANOVA Output

Term	Definition
Groups	Name of groups (variables) included in the analysis
Count	Observations or items (data points) for each variable
Sum	The sum of the values
Average	Arithmetic mean or average for each variable
Variance	Calculated variance for each variable
Source of Variation	Source of error
SS	Sum of squares
df	Degrees of freedom
MS	Mean square
F	Calculated value of the *F* test, referred to as the test statistic
P-value	*p*-value for *F* test
F crit	Critical value for *F* test

Examining the Relationship Between Two Variables (Correlation)

Recall from the previous chapter that correlational analysis allows you to determine if and how two variables are related. That is, you may find that (a) there is no relationship between the two; (b) there is a positive relationship, such that as variable 1 increases so too does variable 2; or (c) there is a negative relationship, such that as variable 1 increases, variable 2 decreases (or vice versa). Excel allows you to mathematically compute this degree of association—and determine its strength and direction—via the Pearson correlation coefficient.

The correlation coefficient, usually denoted as *r* in statistical notation, is a standardized value that can range from -1.00 to +1.00. When evaluating a correlation coefficient, you should take note of its direction and magnitude (Creswell, 2006). Direction is easily assessed via the sign (i.e., positive or negative) of the correlation. An *r* value of -1.00 indicates that two variables are completely correlated in an inverse direction, such that as one variable increases, the second variable decreases in an exactly proportionate amount. In similar fashion, a correlation of 1.00 indicates a positive correlation, such that as one variable increases, the second variable increases in an exactly proportionate amount. A correlation of 0.00 indicates that there is no association between the two variables at all.

Magnitude of association is judged by assessing the absolute value of the correlation (its distance from zero). Cohen's (1992) suggestions regarding effect sizes provide a general yardstick for evaluating degrees of association. That is, r values near .10 reveal a small effect, those centered around .30 indicate a medium effect, and those near .50 and higher indicate a large effect. It is important to note that correlations of .53 and -.53 have the same degree of association, but indicate a different relationship between the variables (i.e., positively vs. negatively correlated). The last caveat, noted in the previous chapter, always bears repeating in a discussion about correlational analysis. That is, correlation does not imply causation; simply because two variables are associated does not mean that one causes the other.

To conduct your own correlational analysis in Excel, use the Data Analysis ToolPak:

1. Select the Data Tab, and click Data Analysis
2. Select Correlation from the list and click OK
3. Click Labels in the first row check box.
4. Click the Output Range button in the output options section and enter the location you want Excel to return the results of the analysis.
5. Click OK for your output.

When you correlate two variables, your output will look like a small table that contains three columns and three rows. The labels of the two variables that you correlated will appear across the top and down the side. Each cell in the table indicates the relationship between two variables. In the Excel output shown in Table 5.4, the first data cell indicates the relationship between variable one (i.e., Age) with itself—a correlation that should not surprise you: 1.0. Notice that variable two correlated with itself (i.e., Item 2) is also 1. The cell of interest to you is the one that computes the association between variable one and variable two (i.e., between Age and Item 2): 0.648181. This value is the Pearson correlation coefficient, so rounding to two decimal places, $r = .65$. Thus, there is a strong, positive relationship between Age and scores on Item 2, such that as Age increases scores on Item 2 also increase.

Table 5.4
Sample Correlation Matrix

	Age	Item 2
Age	1	–
Item 2	0.648181	1

Note: When conducting a correlation analysis in Excel, the output does not provide a *p*-value indicating statistical significance. Therefore, you will need to use additional software to determine if the direction and strength of the correlation is significant.

Reporting and Presenting Your Findings

Representing Your Qualitative Data

Once you have completed the process of qualitative coding, your attention turns to conveying the essence of your analysis through a textual presentation. While you may have listened to hours of taped interviews, read and analyzed pages and pages of transcriptions, and developed and sorted many codes, your charge is to package the entirety of that inquiry into accessible, easily digestible chunks for the reader. To paraphrase Eisenhart (2006), action researchers may have several goals in mind when writing up their qualitative research: (a) richly depicting the very setting and/ or phenomenon under study; (b) using the breadth and depth of the collected data to support concepts, findings, and meanings; (c) representing the range of evidence in the analysis, both confirmatory and discomfirmatory; and (d) revealing "unexpected information, processes, or outcomes that emerge from the researcher's dedication to understanding an unfamiliar situation by interacting directly in it" (p. 572). Your purpose may be centered primarily in one of these strands or it might seek to accomplish elements from each. Regardless of your intent, there are some guidelines for effectively conveying your qualitative research findings.

First, your diligent work to surface the major themes and primary overarching patterns during the analysis phase presents an inherent logical structure for the qualitative write-up. That is, devote significant coverage to each of the major emerging themes, perhaps organizing your writing into sub-sections attuned to each of them. Second, since qualitative data at heart represent the thoughts, perceptions, attitudes, and behaviors of the participants, try to stay as close to the data as possible. Stringer (2007) terms this approach the verbatim principle, wherein you use "terms and concepts drawn from the words of the participants themselves. By doing so they are more likely to capture the meanings inherent in people's experience" (p. 99). Thus, for each main theme or evidence pattern, select illustrative and representative quotations. This approach meshes well with a technique Sagor (2005) recommends, which is to generate two types of "factoids:" statistical (e.g., "Eighty percent of interviewed parents expressed positive comments about the religion textbook series") or illustrative (e.g., "I really thought the book gave good examples; it made my second grader's First Communion prep much more real"). Employing a balance of both types in a qualitative narrative provides a useful mix of summative and delineative information.

A third category of guidelines addresses more practical and operative concerns for representing qualitative data. For example, always check quotes for accuracy when moving from recordings to transcripts to report writing. Also, while you do want the words of your participants to take center stage, your representation should not merely be a series of quotations. Each quote should be sufficiently contextualized so that it makes sense and transitional phrases and introductory leads should be used liberally: "A Saint Michael teacher expressed a differing viewpoint, noting that 'if we can share our successes with the community more often and more forcefully, I think our enrollment would grow.'" Robinson and Lai (2006) note that, to increase the credibility of your qualitative report,

> Quotations may be edited to increase comprehension, but edits should not alter the meaning of the quotation. Edits should be indicated by an appropriate textual convention, for example, square brackets ([ ]) to indicate paraphrasing, or an ellipsis (…) to indicate a deleted selection. (p. 185)

Moreover, they caution, "Do not overuse quotations. The focus of the paragraph should be the point that you are making about the quotation rather than the quotation itself" (p. 185).

Consider the questions in Mini-Lab 5.3 as you evaluate the reporting and presentation of your quantitative and qualitative data.

Mini-Lab 5.3: Reporting and Presenting Your Findings

A clear, detailed, and reader-friendly presentation of your findings takes some practice and revision before it is in final form. Consider these steps as you report your findings.

1. For your qualitative data, have you:
   a. Isolated the primary and most central themes, providing details and examples of each? _____
   b. Stayed close to the data by utilizing the verbatim principle? _____
   c. Checked quotes for accuracy? _____
   d. Used introductory and transitional phrases to link quotes and examples? _____
   e. Achieved a balance between your key points and representative quotes (i.e., not overusing quotations)? _____

2. For your quantitative data, have you:
   a. Provided basic descriptive information, such as the mean, percentages, frequencies, and/or standard deviation? _____
   b. Reported the test statistic (e.g., t value or F value), the degrees of freedom, and the probability level (e.g., $p < .05$ or $p < .01$) for your analysis? _____
   c. Developed an appropriate visual representation of your data, adhering to the guidelines for Tables and Figures? _____

AR Insight

" Being able to communicate results clearly is tough for some people, I know. I benefited from having another person not associated with the course (in my case, my spouse) read every draft. His suggestions made me certain that someone totally unfamiliar with my project could understand what I was trying to convey. "

Tables and Figures

Well-constructed tables and figures are efficient, effective means to convey large amounts of information to your reader in a relatively small space. Nicol and Pexman (1999) set the stage for using tables:

> Tables allow complex data to be expressed in a tidy format. By putting research results in a table, two goals are achieved. First, details of the study are presented so they can be subjected to further analysis. Second, by removing long strings of data from the text, the study can be approached from a broad perspective, using the text to analyze trends and explore the implications of the results. (p. 4)

APA cautions that tables should be integral to the text but should be designed so that they can be understood in isolation" (2010, p. 128). Consider the use of a table only when it adds something new to your data presentation or highlights salient features of that which is presented in text. As such, not every analysis will require a table; use them sparingly. When you do create a table, keep in mind that:

- Every table should have a brief but clear explanatory title.
- Tables should be complementary to your text, but they should have sufficient information so that they can be understood on their own.
- Tables should be numbered in the order in which they are mentioned in the text.
- Do not use suffix letters to name tables: 3a, 3b, 3c; instead use Tables 3, 4, and 5.
- Do not write "the table above" (or below) or "the table on page 27"; refer to each table by its number.
- Use horizontal rather than vertical lines within the table.
- See the APA Table Checklist on p. 150 of the *Publication Manual* (APA, 2010) and pp. 125-150 for additional guidance on table preparation.

Like tables, figures are another tool for conveying data in an engaging and parsimonious manner. Figures include charts, graphs, maps, pictures, or other graphic representations of your data. Many of the same guidelines presented for tables are applicable to figures as well: they should not be redundant with narrative presentation of the data; they should be used sparingly; they should be interpretable as a stand-alone piece of information. Additionally, APA states that "if the figure does not add substantively to the understanding of the paper or duplicates other elements of the paper, it should not be included" (2010, pp. 150-151). When you create a figure, keep in mind that:

- Figures should augment rather than duplicate the text.
- Figures should have elements that are easy to read and should be prepared in the same style as other figures in the same paper (i.e., font size, line weight, etc.).
- Figures should be numbered consecutively in the article in the order in which they are first mentioned in the text.
- Include only one figure per page.
- Figures should be constructed in black and white only. Use textures and shading rather than colors to differentiate bars, lines, and pie segments.
- See the APA (2010) Figure Checklist on p. 167 of the *Publication Manual* and pp. 150-167 for additional guidance on figure preparation.

Descriptive Statistics

Descriptive statistics can be reported simply and directly in the text. Keep in mind, however, the balance between narrative versus tabular presentation. One APA reference text notes that "if you present descriptive statistics in a table or figure, you do not need to repeat them in text, although highlighting particular data in the narrative may be helpful" (2005, p. 69). When including descriptive statistics in the findings, consider examples such as these:

- Of the teachers surveyed, 100% of respondents (12 out of 12) reported that they either *Disagreed* or *Strongly Disagreed* that Saint Michael School has sufficient resources to meet the needs of its students without consolidating.
- The item with the highest level of agreement among parishioner parents (n = 30) related to the importance of the school ministry to Saint Michael Parish (M = 3.50, SD = 0.51).

In those cases when it may be more effective or expedient to convey greater amounts of data via a tabular presentation, you may create variations of the following examples provided in Tables 5.5 and 5.6.

Table 5.5

Mean and Standard Deviation for Stakeholder Responses to School Survey

	Parishioner parent (*n* = 30)		Non-parishioner parent (*n* = 27)		Parishioner non-parent (*n* = 25)		Saint Michael teacher (*n* = 12)	
	M	*SD*	*M*	*SD*	*M*	*SD*	*M*	*SD*
School is an important ministry of the parish	3.50	0.51	2.59	0.57	2.44	0.76	3.67	0.49
Strong connection between parish and school	3.43	0.68	2.44	0.51	2.16	0.68	3.58	0.85
Consolidation will be beneficial for the parish	2.40	1.10	2.48	1.25	2.72	1.06	2.25	1.29
Sufficient resources without consolidation	2.37	0.49	1.93	0.67	1.80	0.65	2.33	0.14
Consolidation will improve the quality of Catholic education	1.80	0.65	1.67	0.48	1.96	0.73	1.42	0.51

Note. * *p* < .01

Table 5.6

Mean, Standard Deviation, Response Count, and Frequency for Survey Questions

Item	*M*	*SD*	*Strongly disagree*	*Disagree*	*Agree*	*Strongly agree*
School is an important ministry of the parish	2.98	0.79	2 (2%)	24 (26%)	42 (45%)	26 (27%)
Strong connection between parish and school	2.83	0.85	4 (4%)	31 (33%)	36 (38%)	23 (25%)
Consolidation will be beneficial for the parish	2.49	1.15	26 (27.7%)	20 (21.3%)	24 (25.5%)	24 (25.5%)
Sufficient resources without consolidation	2.09	0.63	15 (16%)	56 (59%)	23 (25%)	0 (0%)
Consolidation will improve the quality of Catholic education	1.75	0.63	33 (35%)	51 (54%)	10 (11%)	0 (0%)

t Test

A standard way to report most test statistics is to report the general finding, "then report the test statistic, its degrees of freedom and the probability value of that test statistic" (Field, 2009, p. 333). In the case of a *t* test, here are some example results statements:

- Compared to non-parishioners, parishioners at Saint Michael reported significantly higher levels of agreement with the statement that the school has sufficient resources to meet the needs of its students without consolidation, $t(55) = 2.84, p < .01$.
- There was a significant difference between the test scores at Time 1 ($M = 89.2$, $SD = 5.6$) compared to Time 2 ($M = 97.1$, SD = 4.7), $t(57) = 3.14, p < .05$.

Note some commonalities of both statements: the test statistic itself—*t*—is italicized. The parentheses immediately after the *t* contain the number of degrees of freedom, a value obtained from your Excel output. Next you report the actual *t* value itself, followed by the probability level, again noting that the *p* is italicized. If you choose to report the actual means and standard deviations in the text as in the second example, APA requires that you italicize that statistical notation as well (i.e., *M* and *SD*). Table 5.7 provides an example in table form.

Table 5.7
Mean, Standard Deviation, and t-Statistic for Stakeholder Response to Available Resources

Survey Question	Parishioner parent		Non-parishioner parent			
	M	SD	M	SD	df	t-value
Saint Michael School has sufficient resources to meet the needs of its students without consolidating	2.37	0.49	1.92	0.68	55	2.84*

Note. * *p* < .01

ANOVA

The results of an ANOVA can be reported citing the obtained *F* value, the degrees of freedom from the statistical test, and the probability level. For example, here are a few ANOVA results statements. Table 5.8 presents a sample of results in the form of a table.

- The mean Catholic Identity Index values differed across the three sample dioceses, $F(2, 512) = 7.17, p < .01$.
- An analysis of variance, $F(3, 189) = 2.87$, indicated that, over the course of the year, there was a statistically significant ($p < .05$) change in students'

test scores (M at T1 = 56; M at T2 = 67; M at T3 = 88).

- An analysis of variance (ANOVA) revealed significant differences among the key stakeholder groups for three of the questions of interest: Important ministry, $F(3,90) = 22.94$, p < .01; Parish/school connection, $F(3,90) = 28.83$, $p < .01$; and Resources, $F(3,90) = 5.59$, $p < .01$.

Table 5.8

Mean, Standard Deviation, and ANOVA for Stakeholder Responses to School Survey

	Parishioner parent (*n* = 30)		Non-parishioner parent (*n* = 27)		Parishioner non-parent (*n* = 25)		Saint Michael teacher (*n* = 12)		ANOVA
Variable	*M*	*SD*	*M*	*SD*	*M*	*SD*	*M*	*SD*	*F* (3, 90)
School is an important ministry of the parish	3.50	0.51	2.59	0.57	2.44	0.76	3.67	0.49	22.94*
Strong connection between parish and school	3.43	0.68	2.44	0.51	2.16	0.68	3.58	0.85	28.83*
Consolidation will be beneficial for the parish	2.40	1.10	2.48	1.25	2.72	1.06	2.25	1.29	0.59
Sufficient resources without consolidation	2.37	0.49	1.93	0.67	1.80	0.65	2.33	0.14	5.59*
Consolidation will improve the quality of Catholic education	1.80	0.65	1.67	0.48	1.96	0.73	1.42	0.51	2.33

Note. * $p < .01$

Correlation

The results of a correlation are presented either in text or as part of a particular table referred to as a correlation matrix (see Table 5.9). The major components to include in a standard findings statement are the variables being associated via the correlational analysis, the resulting correlation coefficient, and the probability level. For example, here are a few correlational results statements:

- Scores on the High School Placement Test showed a significant positive correlation with high school GPA, $r(145) = .67$, $p < .01$.
- Age was negatively and significantly correlated with parishioners' level of agreement regarding the importance of Saint Michael School to the ministry of the parish, $r = -0.35$, $p < .01$. This association indicates that older parishioners

were less likely to see the importance of the school to the ministry of the parish; similarly, younger parishioners held a more positive view of the ministry of the school to the parish.

Table 5.9
*Correlation Coefficients for Years Affiliated With Parish
and Importance of Saint Michael School to the Parish*

Variable	1	2
1. Number of years affiliated with the parish/school	--	-0.35*
2. Importance of Saint Michael School to the parish	-0.35*	--

Note. * $p < .01$

Summary Guidelines for Findings

Figure 5.3 offers a general template to assist you in describing the content, flow, and organization of your findings section.

Figure 5.3   Outline for Constructing the Findings Section

```
                        Findings Section
  1.  Findings Introduction
        a.   Primary hypotheses or questions of interest
        b.   Experimental design and the tests or methods employed
  2.  Specific Results
        a.   First or most important research question
             i.    (Quantitative)
                   1.   Descriptive statistics for sample (mean, standard deviation,
                        etc.)
                   2.   Statement of specific test (and internal reliability if appropriate)
                   3.   Results of specific test (test statistic, significance, effect size,
                        etc.)
                   4.   Visual representation of data (table, figure, appendix, etc.)
                   5.   Brief comment on individual test results
             ii.   (Qualitative)
                   1.   Statement of specific analysis method
                   2.   Descriptive statistics for sample (percentages, ratios, etc.)
                   3.   Specific themes or categories (quotes, vignettes, etc.)
                   4.   Visual representation of data (table, figure, appendix, etc.)
                   5.   Brief comment on individual test results
        b.   Second or next most important research question
             i.    Repeat steps from above for quantitative and qualitative results
  3.  General Conclusion
        a.   Brief comment on general results
        b.   Brief comment on relationship between and among results
```

Conclusion

The findings section allows you to proffer answers to the animating research questions that gave rise to your action research. While there are different requirements for reporting quantitative and qualitative results, the elements reviewed here are included in the findings section regardless of methodology:

- General introduction to section—often restating your research questions
- Description of analysis and results for each hypothesis or question of interest
- Appropriate format and sufficient detail for quantitative and qualitative results
    - Quantitative components: type of test or analysis run, internal reliability of measure, group means, group standard deviation, test statistics, degrees of freedom, significance level, strength of relationship
    - Qualitative components: type or method of analysis, descriptive statistics for individuals or groups (percentages, ratio, etc.), themes or categories that emerge from data, illustrative quotations, vignettes
- Visual representation of data, such as tables, charts, graphs, models

Action Research in Action:
Findings Section

Design and Procedure

This mixed-method action research project employed a cross-sectional survey and semi-structured interview to address the primary questions of interest. All participants ($N =$ 94) completed the survey instrument, and a sub-sample ($n = 10$) completed the semi-structured interview. Multiple data points (i.e., surveys and interviews) with community stakeholders (i.e., parents, teachers, and parishioners) were used to triangulate and validate the data.

An announcement explaining this action research project appeared in the parish bulletin and school newsletter in September 2010, two weeks after a series of town hall meetings to discuss the proposed consolidation of several local Catholic schools. Interested participants provided their contact information and were mailed a consent form (see Appendix C) and a paper survey to complete at their convenience. Completed surveys and consent forms were returned to the researcher in a self-addressed, stamped envelope. The same sample of participants was contacted independent of the request to complete the survey to participate in an individual interview with the researcher. Interviews were conducted at Saint Michael School in the researcher's office. Interviews were audio recorded and typically lasted between 30 to 45 minutes. Survey and interview data collection was completed by December 2010.

In addition to the survey and interview data, the researcher collected school enrollment data for the past 5 years. This data was used to establish a general trajectory of enrollment trends at Saint Michael School and to address concerns about declining enrollment that were expressed in the survey and interviews.

Findings

The purpose of this action research project was to examine factors that impact the accessibility and affordability of a Saint Michael education, and explore stakeholder perceptions of the proposed consolidation plan. An original survey instrument and semi-structured interviews were used in this mixed-method study. An analysis of variance (ANOVA) was used to analyze the quantitative survey data and open coding techniques were used to identify emergent themes in the semi-structured interview data. Additionally, a basic descriptive analysis was conducted on enrollment data for the past 5 years.

Inferential statistics were used to examine stakeholder responses to four questions on the survey instrument. The ANOVA revealed significant differences among the key stakeholder groups for three of the questions of interest: Important Ministry $F(3,90) = 22.94$, $p < .01$, Parish/School Connection $F(3,90) = 28.83$, $p < .01$, and Resources $F(3,90) = 5.59$, $p < .01$ (see Table 1).

Post hoc comparisons of stakeholder groups within each question revealed the nature of these general between group differences. When asked to indicate their agreement with the statement that Saint Michael School is an important ministry of Saint Michael Parish, parishioner-parents ($M = 3.50$, $SD = 0.51$) and teachers ($M = 3.67$, $SD = 0.57$) indicated significantly higher agreement than both non-parishioner-parents ($M = 2.59$, $SD = 0.76$) and parishioner-non-parents ($M = 2.44$, $SD = 0.49$).... [section continues].

Next, a correlation analysis was conducted to determine the relationship between number of years affiliated with the parish or school and agreement with importance of the ministry of Saint Michael School for the parish (see Table 2). The correlation revealed a significant negative correlation between these variables of interest, $r(94) = -0.35$, $p < .01$. This finding indicates that as years of affiliation increase, agreement with the valuing the ministry of the school decreases. Qualitative data collected from the final three questions of the interview protocol were analyzed using constant comparative coding to complement the primary quantitative analyses. The final questions in the interview protocol asked participants to share their thoughts on the impact of the consolidation, their personal concerns, and any other general thoughts or comments they would like to share. Analysis of the data provided through these questions revealed three major themes: parish-school connection, academic and extracurricular opportunities, and finances.

The most frequent response to the interview questions related to the parish-school

PERSPECTIVES ON CATHOLIC SCHOOL CONSOLIDATION   9

connection (57 text segments). Nearly all participants articulated a sense of loss of an important connection between the parish and the school. A teacher captured this general sentiment when she stated, "Saint Michael School has a great relationship with the parish. I am afraid that this new [consolidated] school will lose the important connection to the parish community." A parent echoed this concern, stating that "[My child] has found a real community here at Saint Michael School. She sees her friends at school during the week and at Mass [and other church functions] on the weekend…this is a special connection that will be lost when the schools combine." These parent and teacher comments reflect a concern that consolidating schools will compromise the important connection between the life of the parish and the school.... [section continues].

Finally, a brief descriptive analysis was conducted on the enrollment data for the past five years at Saint Michael Parish (see Figure 1). Over the past 5 years, enrollment at Saint Michael School has decreased by 11% ($N = 17$). While there was a slight increase in student enrollment from 2006 to 2008, there has been a general downward trend for the past 5 years.

The data from this mixed-method action research project reveal important differences in stakeholder perceptions regarding the proposed consolidation of Saint Michael School. Stakeholders are concerned that the proposed consolidation will compromise or diminish the important parish school connection, but also recognize that there are important benefits to be had in academic and extracurricular activities by consolidating schools. The implication of these findings will be discussed in the following section.

Discussion and Extension

The purpose of this action research project was to explore stakeholder perceptions of the proposed school consolidation plan. An original survey instrument and semi-structured interviews were used in this mixed-method study. The primary analysis of data indicated significant differences among stakeholders' perceptions of the proposed consolidation of Saint Michael School.

6

Discussion and Extension

Thomas (2005) offers a simple way to frame your thinking about the next stage of your action research project, developing the discussion and extension section. Thomas characterizes research as essentially consisting of two phases—description and interpretation. The discussion section falls squarely in the latter domain: "Whereas the descriptive stage tells what happened, the interpretive stage suggests what the happenings mean" (p. 161). The discussion and extension section of the action research paper is where the study findings, their implications, methodological limitations, and next steps are discussed. This chapter will highlight important characteristics of the discussion and extension section and provide guidance on crafting a draft that (a) reviews and contextualizes your findings; (b) presents implications and action steps; (c) reviews study limitations; (d) describes a plan to share your work; and (e) establishes additional action research questions and next steps.

The Discussion and Extension Section

The *Publication Manual of the American Psychological Association* (APA) states that this section provides the researcher an opportunity to "examine, interpret, and qualify the results and draw inferences and conclusions from them" (2010, p. 35). Johnson (2008) echoes the APA recommendations, suggesting that three components comprise this section: conclusions and recommendations, evaluation of the study (limitations, etc.), and designing a new plan or program. Johnson further describes the discussion section as an exercise in reasoned deduction. That is, stepping back from all that data that you have collected, a series of questions are posed: "What does it all mean? What is it that you now know to be true? What can we deduce from the data you have presented?" (p. 128).

Locke, Silverman, and Spirduso (2004) underscore the primary function of the discussion and extension section: "It is in this section that the researcher...gives an answer to the ever-present (if implicit) question, 'So what?'" (p. 205; see also Stringer, 2007, p. 182). These authors call this section the "mother lode" for the reader who is interested not so much in procedures and methodological detail as outcomes. In the discussion and extension section, you will complete the arc of your AR report by responding to the research problem and specific research questions that you established in the introduction and literature review. Note too, that unlike other parts of the report—except perhaps the statement of the problem—it is both likely and permissible that your zeal shows through in crafting this part of the project. In fact, James, Milenkiewicz, and Bucknam (2008) describe this section as

> the place for the passion of the PAR [participatory action research] practitioner to come forth. What is the meaning of this research to the researchers personally, to their practice and the practice of others in their community and district? Does this research have broader implications in the field of education? If so, what are these implications and how does this research justify the conclusion? (p. 182)

What You Asked, What You Found, and How It Fits

The section should begin with a brief restatement of the purpose of the study followed by a review of how the results were obtained and analyzed. Think of this as a brief, 1-3 sentence recap of your design and procedure—the method and analytic tools used to establish your findings. As noted earlier, recall that sometimes readers will go directly to the discussion section to retrieve most expediently the major conclusions of a study. Your efforts to briefly recast the purpose and method provide an immediate framework to couch what follows.

Next you will present your major findings, but now with more contextualizing information and commentary. Unlike in the findings section, where you reported that a correlation existed between two variables, you now restate that finding in more narrative terms and offer interpretation of that relationship. For example, discuss what the relationship or correlation between these particular variables means for your action research project. This exercise is more than restating your findings in narrative form; provide the reader with your interpretation of the findings and what they mean for your study.

Your findings should also be situated back into the literature that you reviewed at the outset of the paper. This includes findings that intuitively fit with and confirm the knowledge base and those that are counterintuitive or contradictory. You should cite additional relevant sources, empirical or theoretical evidence from previous studies, and your own informed, practical experience as you present your interpretation of findings. Mertler and Charles (2008) note that "this is the one place in the report where you are allowed to speculate a bit, to move a little beyond hard evidence and stringent logic" (p. 178). Thus, new understandings and insights gleaned from the action research are featured and placed in the context of existing knowledge (Stringer, 2007).

In addition to discussing all successful or significant findings in the study, you must address areas of the study that were not successful or did not yield significant results. Knowing that a particular program or educational intervention did not work is powerful knowledge. Johnson and Christensen (2004) encourage you to entertain the following questions: "Have alternative explanations for the study results been examined?" and "Do the results conflict with prior research? If they do, has an explanation been provided for the conflicting data?" (p. 87).

Consider the questions in Mini-Lab 6.1 as you continue to pore over your findings and reflect on the meaning or impact they have on your overall research project.

Mini-Lab 6.1: Interpreting Your Findings

1. Are my findings congruent with what I expected to find?
2. How do my findings match up with findings in the literature?
3. What contribution do these findings make to the overall research project?

Implications and Action Planning

Action research is unquestionably dynamic. Your data—and the implications of your findings—are the springboard for action. Scholars are of one accord on this point: "Without action, there is no action research" (Holly, Arhar, & Kasten, 2009, p. 217) and "Designing a new plan or program is putting the action in action research" (Johnson, 2008, p. 136). Johnson highlights the culminating aspect of this part of your project:

> Everything in your action research report leads up to the section in which you discuss your findings and make your conclusions and recommendations based on the data collected. This is followed by what most consider to be the most important part of an action research project—your plan describing actions you will take based on your findings. (p. 128)

Here you grapple with questions such as "What does this work add to my practice or profession?" and "What larger issues in education or Catholic education does this research point to?" Therefore, as action researchers, you must articulate in the discussion and extension section how your research is likely to change practice and/or policy and generate new, vibrant research questions.

After your labors of data collection and analysis, you may be ready to shout, as Mertler amusingly noted: "I've got results!...Now what?" (2009, p. 177). Reasoned action is what should follow, and that plan should be borne out of sustained and critical professional reflection. You were already an insider in your school context when you began your research and now you are an insider with in-depth knowledge of a particular issue (Anderson, Herr, & Nihlen, 1994). Never underestimate, as Anderson and colleagues write, that "as insiders in the system, practitioners have a unique vantage point from which to problem solve" (p. 175). On the heels of your data collection and analysis, that vantage point is evidence-based, data-informed, and action-oriented.

Action planning can take various forms and can unfold on several levels. First, consider that action plans fall along a spectrum from "brief statements or simple descriptions about the implementation of a new educational practice" to a larger, school- or diocesan-wide plan for engaging alternative approaches to addressing the original problem (Mertler, 2009, p. 180). Some action plans are highly formalized, perhaps a brief report to your superintendent, while others are more informal, like a list of recommendations shared at a faculty meeting. Second, depending on the nature and scope of your project, action plans can be focused at an individual, team, school, or diocesan level (Mertler, 2009). For example, recommendations and action steps to improve access to federal IDEA services at the diocesan level are centered more on broader institutional change (Frazier, 2008) than suggesting modifications for a single school's approach to adolescent literacy (Healy, 2008). Regardless of where your action steps fall on the spectrum, remember that they must flow from and be related to your data. Avoid making overly generalized or grandiose claims that extend beyond what can be supported by the data in your study.

While you should be cautious about understating or overstating your action steps based on just one research project (James et al., 2008), enlisting the professional input of colleagues and administrators helps to strategize responses that are in line with your findings. In addition, a simple framework offered by Stringer (2007) is useful regardless of how formal or informal your ultimate action may be. Based around key interrogative questions, the guide for action planning has six parts:

- **Why**—The goal you want to achieve.
- **What**—Your objective(s) for reaching that goal.
- **How**—The specific tasks that lead to each objective.
- **Who**—The people necessary to conduct the tasks and reach each objective.
- **Where**—The place in which the work will occur.
- **When**—The estimated timeline for conducting tasks, completing objectives, and meeting the ultimate goal (see Stringer, 2007, pp. 128-129).

Now that you have collected and analyzed your data and begun to articulate the importance of your findings, what recommendations will you offer? Complete Mini-Lab 6.2 to assist with these next steps in your AR report.

Mini-Lab 6.2: Now What?

As you begin to formulate action steps based on your research findings, consider the following questions:

1. What kinds of recommendations (formal or informal) best suit your action research project and specific findings?
2. At what level are these recommendations most appropriate, relevant, and useful (classroom, school, diocesan, other)?

Articulating and accounting for the required resources is another important consideration. The power of articulating an action plan is that the "teacher-researcher now has some sort of strategy for trying out, carrying out, or otherwise putting into practice the changes resulting from the findings of an action research project" (Mertler, 2009, p. 180). You do not have to go at this alone; now is an opportune time to engage school colleagues as collaborators and work together to implement the recommendations flowing from your action research project.

Limitations

Every piece of research has limitations. Every researcher, at the end of a study, knows that they would handle some situations differently if they had it all to do over again. The discussion and extension section requires that you delineate those observations. Via reflection, you should consider the strengths and weaknesses of your methodology, design, and analysis as well as reconsider the original questions posed and the nature and quality of the answers that you arrived at. You have an opportunity to provide a clear and forthright recounting of obstacles, difficulties, and "errors you inadvertently made, problems you encountered unexpectedly" (Mertler & Charles, 2008, p. 178). In so doing, you can conceive of the limitations section as an act of thoughtful, critical, and objective professional evaluation of your action research.

Figure 6.1 lists several categories to consider when discussing the limitations of your research, covering major study elements such as participants, instruments, design, and statistics. Choose only those components that are applicable to your study—not all categories or components will necessarily apply. Remember, most limitations will address weaknesses in the specific methods of your research that affect the claims you are able to make about your findings.

Figure 6.1   Categories to Consider When Discussing Limitations of Your Research

Category	Components to Consider for Limitations	
Participants	**Sample**	Did you omit or neglect to assess key stakeholder groups? Does your sample accurately reflect the population you are studying?
	Response rate	Did you receive a low response to your survey or questionnaire?
Instruments	**Validity**	Did your survey or questionnaire have sufficient content and construct validity? Did you really measure what you say you were measuring?
Design	**Procedure and analysis**	Were there any potential issues with how you implemented your project or intervention? Did the timing or ordering of activities impact your results? Did you choose the appropriate method of analysis (quantitative, qualitative, or both) to address your questions of interest?
Statistics	**Tests**	Did you conduct the specific test or statistical analysis that was appropriate for your questions of interest?

AR Insight

As you begin to consider the limitations of your study, remember that not everything is a limitation. Often as you look back at your project you will see many things that you would have changed or done differently, but these changes may not in fact compromise the integrity of your research. For example, a small sample size is not a limitation if the intent of your project was to examine the impact of an innovative afterschool reading program at your school. If the entire afterschool program is small in number (say 15 kids), and you interview all of them, you have indeed engaged the appropriate population, but could not increase your sample size even if you wanted to. There simply are no more students at your school who fit the selection criteria. In fact, in this instance, adding more students from your school who are not in the afterschool program would confound your findings and would itself be a limitation.

Dissemination

There is a responsibility that comes with action research that must not be shirked or shortchanged. Namely, it is critical that you make plans to share and disseminate your work. The theme of Christian community—so much at the heart of Catholic schools—

is bound up in this type of professional sharing and building of collegiality (Frabutt, Holter, & Nuzzi, 2008; Moore, 2004; Sacred Congregation for Catholic Education, 1982). Consider the metaphor offered by Dana and Yendol-Silva (2003) encouraging teacher researchers to distribute their inquiry broadly; they wrote:

> An unshared teacher inquiry is like the stone lying beside the pond. Unless that inquiry is tossed into the professional conversation and dialogue that contributes to the knowledge base for teaching, the inquiry has little chance of creating change. However, once tossed in, the inquiry disturbs the status quo of educational practices, creating a ripple effect, beginning with the teacher himself or herself and his or her immediate vicinity (the students and his or her classroom) and emanating out to a school, a district, a state, eventually reaching and contributing to the transformation of the perimeter of all practice—the profession of teaching itself. (pp. 139-140)

Their admonition, like ours to you today, is to ensure that you "get into the pond" (p. 140).

Multiple venues exist for communicating your research to others. Start at the local level by presenting your research to the faculty, administrators, and colleagues in your school. Your work might be shared as part of a general faculty meeting, a unit level meeting, or within the context of a professional development session. In some cases, action research findings contribute directly to existing faculty work groups such as accreditation committees or school improvement teams. Beyond your own school, your research holds the potential to inform other similarly situated faculty and administrators. Thus, conference presentation venues like the National Catholic Educational Association annual meeting, Notre Dame's annual Mary Ann Remick Leadership Conference, and regional gatherings of Catholic educators are appropriate for showcasing your work. Other outlets include academic journals, professional newsletters, or online action research journals.

Thomas (2005) offers a dissemination list that is broader and more comprehensive than most. Each of the items in Figure 6.2 represents a unique way that you can cast your stone into the pond. In the end, be reminded that "This act of sharing—and, in fact, *celebrating*—the findings of your action research can actually be a very satisfying and rewarding *professional* experience" (Mertler, 2009, p. 193). Consider how you will share your work with colleagues and stakeholders by completing Mini-Lab 6.3. See Appendix B for more information on opportunities and venues for disseminating your research, and instructions for creating a compelling research brief.

Mini-Lab 6.3: Sharing Your Research

Consider three specific opportunities to present your research at the school, diocesan, or community level.

Figure 6.2   Ideas for Dissemination (from Thomas, 2005)

Venues/Means for Action Research Project Dissemination
Oral presentation at a faculty meeting
Article in the school newspaper
Item in a newsletter distributed to members of an education association
Bulletin issued by a school district or a university research bureau
Teacher's master's-degree thesis or doctoral dissertation
Paper delivered at an educational conference
Report presented at a university seminar
Item in a daily newspaper or weekly newsmagazine
Item on a radio or television news hour
Article in a professional journal
Entry on an Internet Web site
Chapter in a book
An entire book

Next Steps/Future Directions

The last piece of your discussion and extension section is forward-looking, offering a vision of what should come next. In a sense, this concluding endeavor in your project is not really a terminus at all; what it illustrates is that "action research never really ends; the professional educator continues to move through subsequent cycles throughout his or her career, always searching for ways to improve educational and instructional practice" (Mertler, 2009, pp. 181-182). Hendricks' (2006) comment that "the next stage of the action research process is one of renewing or beginning again" should remind you of the continuous recursive cycle of the action research loop (p. 150).

You have fully completed one cycle of research, arriving at a new plateau with deeper knowledge and more sophisticated understanding, but questions no doubt remain or new ones have arisen. If the behavioral intervention that you evaluated was found to be largely effective, how can it be improved? If the professional development model that you studied was shown to be ineffective in meeting its goals, how will you investigate finding its replacement? If you explored strategies to engage Latino parishioners more directly in your school, how will you now measure the impact of the new outreach initiatives? In each example, your diligent inquiry has brought you to a new point of departure that demands another action research journey. Taking stock of all that has transpired, "now the process begins anew as you reflect on what you have learned and use that information for ongoing reflective planning" (Hendricks, 2006, p. 150).

What new and compelling questions have emerged from your AR project? Complete Mini-Lab 6.4 and articulate these new questions and next steps.

Mini-Lab 6.4: New Questions

Action research is a recursive process; the successful completion of each loop will generate new questions of interest. Consider three new and engaging questions that flow from your current AR project.

Summary Guidelines for Discussion and Extension

In many ways, the discussion and extension section ties your action research together and offers a glimpse into the future. Figure 6.3 is a template to use as a general guide when constructing your discussion and extension section.

Figure 6.3   Outline for Constructing the Discussion Section

Discussion Section

1. Discussion and Extension Introduction
   a. Brief overview of the purpose of the study
   b. Brief review of how the results were obtained and analyzed
2. Implications and Application of Specific Results
   a. What do the major findings or results mean?
      i. Interpret the data
      ii. Articulate the implications of these results
      iii. Examine them in light of the literature reviewed earlier in the paper
   b. How can the findings be applied to your practice and/or profession?
      i. Infer policy or practice changes given these results or findings
      ii. Entertain the implications of these changes
   c. How will you share your results and conclusions with colleagues?
      i. Discuss plan to share results with colleagues and stakeholders
3. Limitations of the Study (see Figure 6.1)
   a. What were the known weaknesses of the study?
   b. What changes could be made to reduce these problems?
4. Future Directions
   a. What new, vibrant questions of interest does your study produce?
   b. Based on your research, what is the next loop in the action research sequence?
5. General Conclusion
   a. Comment on the overall importance of your action research project
   b. Address one or more of the questions presented in the above prompt

AR Insight

" Although the process of action research may seem daunting at times, it will yield great benefits for your school and other Catholic schools. Action research is worth the effort! "

Conclusion

Much attention has been given to the chasm between educational research and practice, and there are those that have championed action research as an approach to bridge that divide (Frabutt et al., 2008). More so than any previous section, the discussion and extension section has the potential to solidify the research-practice connection. Carefully recounting your findings, interpreting them with both precision and passion, linking them to extant educational research, and recommending a viable action plan all contribute to a transformative kind of inquiry that is both research-based and action-oriented. As you craft and review your discussion and extension section, be cognizant that ultimately it should depict the full arc of your project, for "the final measure of your action research is the degree to which it clearly asks and answers your question, communicates your ideas, and serves to promote positive change" (Johnson, 2008, p. 138).

Action Research in Action:
Discussion and Extension Section

connection (57 text segments). Nearly all participants articulated a sense of loss of an important connection between the parish and the school. A teacher captured this general sentiment when she stated, "Saint Michael School has a great relationship with the parish. I am afraid that this new [consolidated] school will lose the important connection to the parish community." A parent echoed this concern, stating that "[My child] has found a real community here at Saint Michael School. She sees her friends at school during the week and at Mass [and other church functions] on the weekend…this is a special connection that will be lost when the schools combine." These parent and teacher comments reflect a concern that consolidating schools will compromise the important connection between the life of the parish and the school.... [section continues].

Finally, a brief descriptive analysis was conducted on the enrollment data for the past five years at Saint Michael Parish (see Figure 1). Over the past 5 years, enrollment at Saint Michael School has decreased by 11% ($N = 17$). While there was a slight increase in student enrollment from 2006 to 2008, there has been a general downward trend for the past 5 years.

The data from this mixed-method action research project reveal important differences in stakeholder perceptions regarding the proposed consolidation of Saint Michael School. Stakeholders are concerned that the proposed consolidation will compromise or diminish the important parish school connection, but also recognize that there are important benefits to be had in academic and extracurricular activities by consolidating schools. The implication of these findings will be discussed in the following section.

Discussion and Extension

The purpose of this action research project was to explore stakeholder perceptions of the proposed school consolidation plan. An original survey instrument and semi-structured interviews were used in this mixed-method study. The primary analysis of data indicated significant differences among stakeholders' perceptions of the proposed consolidation of Saint Michael School.

Discussion of Major Findings

As expected, the descriptive analysis of enrollment data revealed a general decline in enrollment over the past five years (11% overall). The decline in enrollment does not represent a large number (only 17 students), nor is it as drastic as other schools in the area (i.e., Saint Stanislaus and Sacred Heart enrollments have declined 25% and 27% respectively over the same time period). However, with multiple Catholic schools in the urban core experiencing similar trends, action steps must be taken to remediate this marked decline (McDonald & Schultz, 2010). Consolidation is one such option to address the overall issue of declining enrollment in urban Catholic schools across the country. Yet, there are some concerns among key stakeholder groups about the impact of school consolidation on the parish and school community. Parishioner-parents and teachers—stakeholders with distinct personal and professional connections to the parish and school—indicated the highest agreement with the importance of Saint Michael School to the parish. Said another way, individuals with the greatest personal and professional investment in the school were more likely to see its value to the overall ministry of the parish. Furthermore, these same stakeholders were concerned that consolidation will abrogate the important and life-giving relationship that currently exists between the parish and the school.

However, school consolidation is not without benefits. Increasing enrollment through consolidation would provide additional income to the school that could be used to expand academic programs and extracurricular activities. These economies of scale provide financial advantages that, properly managed, can have positive impact on the educational opportunities at the school (Ash, 2007; Dodson & Garrett, 2004). Participants who were interviewed for this study acknowledged these potential benefits—yet, some seemed hesitant to admit that the benefits of consolidation could outweigh the cost to the parish and school community.

Application of Findings

This action research project has revealed that there are strong and varied opinions on the proposed consolidation of St Michael Catholic School. These stakeholder opinions provide valuable insight into the perceived importance and viability of Catholic education in this community. Therefore, it is my recommendation that this study should be replicated in all school and parish communities affected by the proposed plan for consolidation. Once the school- and parish-based replication has been completed, town-hall style meetings and listening sessions can be held to engage and inform all school stakeholders. This systematic and comprehensive approach to seeking information from persons interested and invested in local Catholic education will ensure that the personnel responsible for recommending school closure and consolidation will have the most accurate, reliable, and representative data to inform their decisions.

In addition to providing important information regarding the proposed consolidation of local Catholic schools, this action research project highlighted a concerning disparity in stakeholders' perception of the value of the school to the overall ministry of the parish. While the cause of this disparity is unclear (e.g., no children in the parish school, concern over the financial impact of the school on other parish ministries, etc.), school and parish personnel must redouble their efforts to inform all parishioners that the high quality, faith-filled education provided at St. Michael school is integral to the overall educative mission of the Church. Parishioner understanding and support of a robust education in the faith through our Catholic schools is essential to the long-term viability of Catholic education in this community, regardless of what happens with the proposed consolidation.

Dissemination

The results and final research report of this AR project will be shared with the pastor of Saint Michael Parish and the Saint Michael School Board at their spring meeting in May 2011. A five-page research brief will also be prepared for dissemination among study participants and used in town-hall style meetings with other key stakeholders as the principal and school board members continue to investigate the potential impact of school consolidation on Saint Michael

Parish and School.

Limitations

A limitation of the study arose from the sampling technique used to solicit participants for the study. An announcement of the study was printed in the parish bulletin and school newsletter; anyone interested in the study was asked to participate. This convenience sample may not accurately represent all stakeholder groups since individuals with strong feelings or interest in the issue of consolidation could have been more motivated to respond. The fact that 86% of teachers (12 out of 14) responded to the open invitation speaks to this limitation—no other group had such a high response rate or such a tangible professional investment in the issue of consolidation. This limitation could be mitigated in future studies by identifying stakeholders from parish and school rosters rather than relying solely on the personal interest and initiative of participants.

Future Directions

Designing and implementing this study with key stakeholders in the parish and school community has been an insightful and rewarding process. Asking participants to share their thoughts and feelings on an issue so central to my professional responsibilities and so integral to the parish community has inspired this researcher to collaborate with other principals of schools targeted for this consolidation. Beginning in September 2011, this researcher will work with two other principals to design an AR project that addresses the same research questions in two other parishes in the urban core. These results will then be compared to the data collected in this AR project at Saint Michael Parish and School.

For nearly 200 years the parish school has served as the "privileged environment in which Christian education is carried out" (Congregation for Catholic Education, 1998, para. 11). Seen through this lens, the parish school is a vital and vibrant component of parish life wherein the young receive an education inspired by Christ and nurtured through a distinct and tangible

PERSPECTIVES ON CATHOLIC SCHOOL CONSOLIDATION   13

connection to the larger Church. The proposed consolidation of Saint Michael School is about

more than moving buildings or changing the governance model of an organization—it speaks to

the fundamental importance of Christian education to the overall life and ministry of the parish.

7

Front Material

The two first pages of your action research paper—that fateful first impression that you make on your reader—are the title page and the abstract. Because of their prominence and since certain specific conventions guide the content and formatting of each, this section describes the expectations for developing them.

The Title Page

The first page of your final research paper is much more than a catchy title. Although an engaging title is important, there are a host of other important and required features for this page as specified by the *Publication Manual for the American Psychological Association* (APA; 2010).

Running Head

APA describes the running head as "an abbreviated title that is printed at the top of the pages of a published article to identify the article for readers. The running head should be a maximum of 50 characters, counting letters, punctuation, and spaces between words" (2010, p. 229). The running head is placed flush left within the header opposite the page number. The short title itself is placed in all capital letters, although the words "running head" are not. For example, Running head: STUDENT PERCEPTIONS OF CATHOLIC IDENTITY.

The phrase "Running head" appears only on the first page of the paper. All subsequent pages will contain the short title, left justified within the header, across from the page number. Begin the title page with the number 1; all remaining pages are numbered consecutively from the title page.

Title

The APA Manual notes that the "title should summarize the main idea simply and, if possible, with style" (2010, p. 23). Effective titles concisely telegraph the content of the study. The title encapsulates the central topic of your action research and might invoke the major variables that you considered. For example, "Using Information Technology to Foster Cooperative Learning and Peer Assessment" (Ng, 2008) clearly conveys the main topic area—education and technology—along with the major dependent variables of interest—cooperative learning and peer assessment. APA further recommends the following guidelines in developing a title:

- Centered and double-spaced
- Use uppercase and lowercase letters as appropriate
- Ten to 12 words
- Avoid abbreviations
- Avoid the use of common or superfluous phrases such as "An Investigation of…" or "A Qualitative Study of…"
- Title should easily contract into a shortened form for the header and the running head

Name and Affiliation

Author name and affiliation are entered after the title, double spaced, and in the center of the page. APA recommends first name, middle initial(s), and last name as the preferred author format. Additional titles and degrees are not included. Immediately below your name, on the next double spaced line, include your institutional affiliation (e.g., local school, university, or both).

The Abstract

Placed prominently at the beginning of the paper, immediately after the title page, is the abstract. According to APA, "an abstract is a brief, comprehensive summary of the contents of the article" (2010, p. 25). This concise overview can be likened to an executive summary—providing a glimpse of the action research problem, questions, purpose, methods, findings, and implications (Robinson & Lai, 2006). Dense and descriptive, the abstract should be information-rich. The imagery provided by Locke, Silverman, and Spirduso (2004) is helpful: "The abstract is a portal of entry into the full report" (p. 178). Since "a well-prepared abstract can be the most important single paragraph in your article," care must be taken to draft it effectively (APA, p. 26).

What makes the abstract such a critical piece of your action research paper? Think back to when you first began to investigate your topic and you initiated your literature review search. Often when perusing online databases or conducting library searches, the abstract was the first piece of information about a particular study that you encountered. Based on your consideration of the abstract, you likely made an immediate decision about whether you wanted to read the full article, whether you should download a copy, or whether you wanted to track down other work by the same author (Johnson & Christensen, 2004). You likely made a judgment, based on the abstract, whether the article in question was relevant, appropriate, and worthy of further consideration for your review purposes. Robinson and Lai (2006) make similar observations about the importance of the abstract:

> Since important decisions may be made about your research on the basis of the abstract alone, it is important to write it well. Colleagues will decide whether the study is of sufficient relevance and interest to read the whole report, funding agencies could decide on the basis of your abstract whether to provide further funding, and conference organizers will use the abstract to decide whether your work deserves a place in the program. (p. 179)

Writing Your Abstract

APA (2010) guidelines limit the abstract to a single paragraph ranging from 150-250 words. Moreover, APA recommends that the abstract be accurate, self-contained, concise, and specific. Building on guidelines from Sagor (2005), develop a five-sentence abstract that addresses these major components:

- Initial statement of the action research problem or issue
- Description of the research context
- Overview of the research methodology, briefly mentioning participants and measures
- A summary statement of the most important findings
- Concluding sentence stating implications, action plans, or next steps

It is no doubt challenging to convey all that you want to say—covering the points outlined above—without exceeding the 150-250 word limit. Once you have composed a sentence that addresses each of the components above, some editing and paring back of the text will be necessary so that you do not exceed the word count. As you self-evaluate your completed abstract, ensure that you can answer in the affirmative to each of the prompts offered by Gay, Mills, and Airasian (2009): "Is the problem stated? Are the number and type of participants and instruments described? Is the design identified? Are procedures described? Are the major results and conclusions stated?" (p. 536).

Voice and Tense

As you begin to craft these introductory components for your action research paper you may encounter some unease or confusion as you attempt to find the appropriate language and voice to write about your research. Unlike traditional research or standard academic writing, the first person voice is often appropriate when writing your AR report (see Mertler, 2009, pp. 214-215). You may find yourself using phrases such as "The researcher administered the survey" (i.e., third person) or "when conducting interviews with students I used a semi-structured protocol" (i.e., first person). Whichever voice you choose (i.e., first or third person), make every effort to remain consistent throughout the text.

Verb tense is another potentially tricky grammatical negotiation in AR writing. Even though traditional research reports are typically written in the past tense, there are occasions in your AR report where present or future tense is warranted and preferred (see Mertler, 2009, p. 216). In general, use past tense when writing about research or procedural elements that have already been completed (e.g., literature review, method, and findings section). Present tense can be used in the introduction of your AR report as you are describing educational issues or contextual factors in your school that are current, in progress, or ongoing. However, once you begin to discuss the implications of your findings, make policy recommendations, articulate a dissemination protocol, or offer new and vibrant research questions, it may be more appropriate to use the future tense.

As you negotiate these grammatical and stylistic components of AR writing, remember that consistency is key. Frequently switching voice or using competing tenses will obscure the content and diminish the impact of your writing.

Action Research in Action:
Front Material

Running head: PERSPECTIVES ON CATHOLIC SCHOOL CONSOLIDATION   1

Stakeholder Perspectives on the Consolidation of Saint Michael Catholic School

Theresa Q. Principal

Saint Michael Catholic School

University of Notre Dame

Abstract

Saint Michael Catholic Parish and School are situated in the urban center of a large, Midwestern city that has experienced marked demographic changes over the past several decades. Declining enrollment and unmet capital improvement needs threaten the viability of the school; other local Catholic schools are facing similar enrollment and financial challenges. As such, the diocese has proposed the consolidation of several local Catholic schools into one inter-parish school that will be housed in an existing, centrally located school building. This action research project used a mixed-method action research design to examine stakeholder ($N = 94$) perspectives regarding the proposed consolidation. Surveys and individual interviews were conducted with school parents, parishioners, and school teachers. Results indicated that stakeholders with connections to the parish and school (e.g., a parishioner whose child attends the school) rate the importance of the school to the ministry of the parish higher than stakeholders with less connection to both the parish and school (e.g., a parishioner who does not have children enrolled in the school). Additionally, stakeholders are generally concerned that consolidating the school will abrogate the important relationship between the parish and the school.

8

Concluding Thoughts

Congratulations! You've just written a compelling report chronicling your innovative AR project. In so doing, you have engaged pressing needs and issues in your school community with rigor and systematic research methodology to evince real, positive change for the students you serve, for the school you lead, and for the ministry of Catholic education. Having completed this AR project and report, you know that action research in Catholic education extends beyond any singular research question or course requirement. Said another way, action research in Catholic education is an orientation to leadership that views "working toward the common good...as working for the building up of the Kingdom of God" (Vatican Council II, 1965, para. 60).

The work of building the Kingdom of God through leadership in Catholic education requires dedication and grace, excellence and humility, dogged determination and undying faith. You know these requirements well. You know, too, that this hard work of action research does not provide quick or easy answers to the myriad contemporary issues facing our Catholic schools.

While no single project can address every issue in Catholic education, it is our sincere hope that through the process of action research you have recognized your capacity to address *one* issue, and to do so with skill and acumen. It is through your continued good work to build the Kingdom of God through leadership in Catholic education that our Catholic schools "become an especially powerful instrument of hope" (Benedict XVI, 2008, para. 3).

9

Sample Action Research Report

Note. We want to draw your attention to an important stylistic difference affecting tables and figures in this text. All tables and figures in the Sample Action Research Report—portions at the end of each chapter and the complete sample at the end of the text—are in compliance with the style requirements of the 6th edition of the Publication Manual of the American Psychological Association (APA; 2010). However, tables and figures in the text that are outside of the Sample Action Research Report have been formatted to match the general theme and style of the book, and are not in APA format. Look to examples in the Sample Action Research Report when crafting your own APA compliant tables and figures; do NOT replicate those in the body of the book.

TITLE PAGE: Contains the words "Running head" with title in all caps (50 characters or less), included in header and left justified on the same line as the page number; your title centered and capitalized; your name; your school; your university affiliation.

Running head: PERSPECTIVES ON CATHOLIC SCHOOL CONSOLIDATION   1

TITLE PAGE
(APA, 2010, pp. 23-24, 229)

Stakeholder Perspectives on the Consolidation of Saint Michael Catholic School

Theresa Q. Principal

Saint Michael Catholic School

University of Notre Dame

ABSTRACT: Begins on a new page with a centered, capitalized title. Text is arranged in a single paragraph in block form with no indentation, and can range from 150 to 250 words. Abbreviations and numbers are permitted in the abstract, except to start a sentence.

PERSPECTIVES ON CATHOLIC SCHOOL CONSOLIDATION   2

Abstract

Saint Michael Catholic Parish and School are situated in the urban center of a large, Midwestern city that has experienced marked demographic changes over the past several decades. Declining enrollment and unmet capital improvement needs threaten the viability of the school; other local Catholic schools are facing similar enrollment and financial challenges. As such, the diocese has proposed the consolidation of several local Catholic schools into one inter-parish school that will be housed in an existing, centrally located school building. This action research project used a mixed-method action research design to examine stakeholder ($N = 94$) perspectives regarding the proposed consolidation. Surveys and individual interviews were conducted with school parents, parishioners, and school teachers. Results indicated that stakeholders with connections to the parish and school (e.g., a parishioner whose child attends the school) rate the importance of the school to the ministry of the parish higher than stakeholders with less connection to both the parish and school (e.g., a parishioner who does not have children enrolled in the school). Additionally, stakeholders are generally concerned that consolidating the school will abrogate the important relationship between the parish and the school.

ABSTRACT
(APA, 2010, pp. 25-27)

INTRODUCTION: Begins after the abstract on a new page under the centered, capitalized, full title of the research paper. Does not require an additional heading—the function of this section is conveyed by its position in the paper. Text is arranged in a series of indented paragraphs.

PURPOSE STATEMENT: Begins immediately after the introduction with a new paragraph under the left-justified, boldface heading.

PERSPECTIVES ON CATHOLIC SCHOOL CONSOLIDATION   3

Stakeholder Perspectives on the Consolidation of Saint Michael Catholic School

INTRODUCTION (APA, 2010, pp. 27-28; Creswell, 2008, pp. 68-87)

The landscape of Catholic schools has changed quite dramatically in the past 50 years; personnel, student enrollment, and the overall number of schools have experienced marked change. At their zenith in the 1960s, Catholic schools enrolled over 5 million students in nearly 13,000 schools across the United States. These schools were staffed and led almost entirely by women and men religious. For the 2009-2010 academic year, Catholic schools enrolled approximately 2.12 million students in just over 7,000 K-12 schools—less than half of the schools and students from just five decades ago (McDonald & Schultz, 2010). What's more, these schools are now almost entirely staffed by lay women and men.

Saint Michael Catholic School has not been invulnerable to the enrollment and staffing issues affecting Catholic schools nationally. Situated in the urban center of a large, Midwestern city, Saint Michael School and Parish has experienced significant change since its founding over 130 years ago.... [section continues].

PURPOSE STATEMENT (APA, 2010, p. 28; Creswell, 2008, pp. 54-55, 68-87, 121, 133-146)

Purpose Statement

The purpose of this action research project was to explore stakeholder perceptions of the proposed school consolidation plan.

Research Questions

The major research questions considered in this action research project were:

RESEARCH QUESTIONS (Creswell, 2008, pp. 121, 133-146)

1. What do stakeholders at Saint Michael School and Parish identify as primary concerns or issues regarding the impact of school consolidation on their school and parish community?

2. What is the 5-year enrollment trend at Saint Michael School?

Literature Review

With a net loss of over 1,000 Catholic schools in the last decade alone, Catholic schools are increasingly faced with important decisions about consolidation and closure (McDonald

RESEARCH QUESTIONS: Begin after the purpose statement with a new paragraph under the left-justified, boldface heading. Questions can be bulleted or enumerated for clarity.

LITERATURE REVIEW: Begins immediately after the research questions with a new paragraph under the left-justified, boldface heading. Arranged in a series of indented paragraphs. Each major research theme can be indicated by an indented and boldface heading.

PERSPECTIVES ON CATHOLIC SCHOOL CONSOLIDATION   4

& Schultz, 2010). The following literature review addresses three primary themes to better understand the foundation of and contemporary challenges facing Catholic schools: Church documents on Catholic education, Catholic school statistics, and school consolidation.

> **LITERATURE REVIEW** (APA, 2010, p. 28; Creswell, 2008, pp. 53-54, 88-119)

    Church documents on Catholic education. Catholic schools in the United States comprise a unique context wherein in the sacred and secular commingle. As such, Catholic schools are the "privileged environment in which Christian education is carried out" (Congregation for Catholic Education, 1998, para. 11). Since the Third Plenary Council of Baltimore in 1884, Catholic religious and laypersons have relied on the parish school to serve as the primary provider of this privileged educational environment (Walch, 2003). In response to the perceived prejudice and mistreatment of Catholic children attending the Common public school, U.S. Bishops encouraged all parishes to build schools, and all Catholic parents to send their children to these new parish schools (McCluskey, 1964). Walch (2003) stated,

> Catholic parents had a moral responsibility to provide for the spiritual lives of their
>
> children, and the best means of providing that spiritual life was through parish schools.
>
> Catholic parents were never *required* to send their children to parish schools until 1884,
>
> but not to do so was to incur the displeasure of the organized church. (p. 32)

Though the need for and importance of an education rooted in our Catholic faith has not dissipated, the one-parish-one-school model established over 200 years ago has waned in recent decades.... [section continues].

    Catholic school statistics. The most recent annual report from the National Catholic Educational Association (NCEA; McDonald & Schultz, 2010) indicated that in the last year alone 174 Catholic schools were closed or consolidated. Accounting for new school openings in the same time period (24), there was a net loss of 150 schools. Over the past six decades, the net effect of school consolidation and closing has yielded a loss of over 5,000 schools and 3.10 million students (McDonald & Schultz, 2010). These trends have empowered leaders in the Church and educational research to wonder what new and innovative models might address these dramatic changes in our Catholic educational system (Golway, 2007; Hamilton, 2008; McLaughlin, O'Keefe, & O'Keeffe, 1996). Despite growing evidence that Catholic schools provide civic and financial benefits at the local and national level, many face consolidation and closure (Brinig & Garnett, 2009; Green, 2011).... [section continues].

School consolidation. School consolidation is not a new phenomenon in the United States. Over the past seven decades, average public school enrollment has increased from roughly 100 students per school to 500 students per school (National Education Statistics, 2010). Economies of scale (e.g., leveraging buying power of larger school districts and schools) and reduced administrative costs (e.g., fewer building- and district-level administrators) are often cited as the benefits of consolidating schools in states and school districts across the U.S. (Ash, 2007; Dodson & Garrett, 2004). There are costs associated with consolidation, too. Since 1930, the percentage of school-age children who ride the bus to school has increased from 10% to 60% (Kileen & Sipple, 2000). In addition to the financial costs, a growing body of research indicates that smaller schools may actually serve students better academically and provide more educational opportunities (Lee & Smith, 1997). Lee and Loeb (2000) stated that "a crucial element of any school's structure is the number of students enrolled, that is, the size of the school," which can have an impact on teachers and students alike (p. 4).... [section continues].

A tension exists between the centrality of Catholic schools to the Church's education apostolate, and the financial and demographic realities that threaten the feasibility of many parish schools. While the canon of official Church documents extols the prominence and value of Catholic education, the number of U.S. Catholic schools has been in precipitous decline for the past five decades. School consolidation is one option that increasing numbers of parishes and schools are considering as an alternative to school closure. Though a promising option, school consolidation is not without complications and concessions.

METHOD: Begins with a new, indented paragraph immediately after the literature review under the centered, boldface heading. Always written in past tense as you are referring to work you have already completed.

PARTICIPANTS: Begins with a new indented paragraph under the left-justified, boldface heading.

INSTRUMENTS AND MATERIALS: Follows participants section with a new, indented paragraph under the left-justified, boldface heading. May be separated into relevant subsections similar to the subsections in the literature review, beginning with an indented, boldface heading ending with a period.

PERSPECTIVES ON CATHOLIC SCHOOL CONSOLIDATION   6

Method

The purpose of this action research project was to explore stakeholder perceptions of the proposed school consolidation plan. An original survey instrument and semi-structured interviews were used in this mixed-method study.

Participants

Participants ($N = 94$) were 30 parishioner-parents of current students (10 male, 20 female), 27 non-parishioner-parents of current students (9 male, 18 female), 25 parishioners without school-age children (9 male, 16 female), and 12 teachers (3 male, 9 female). Participants had between 3 and 30 years of affiliation with the parish or school ($M = 16.7$ years affiliation; $SD = 6.1$). All participants were selected from a convenience sample of individuals who responded to an announcement in the parish bulletin and school newsletter.

Instruments and Materials

Survey instrument. An original survey instrument was used to assess stakeholder perceptions of access to an education at Saint Michael School and general thoughts on the proposed school consolidation (see Appendix A). The survey instrument consisted of five statements and a corresponding 4-point Likert scale ranging from *Strongly Agree* (1) to *Strongly Disagree* (4). Participants were asked to indicate their level of agreement or disagreement with questions such as "The proposed school consolidation will be beneficial for Saint Michael Parish."

Interview protocol. An original interview protocol was used in this study to engage stakeholders at Saint Michael Parish and School in questions regarding the impact of consolidation on their community (see Appendix B). The semi-structured interview protocol consisted of five open-ended questions that addressed affiliation with the school and perception of the consolidation. Participants were asked to respond to questions such as "What is your biggest concern regarding the proposed consolidation?"

METHOD
(APA, 2010, pp. 29-32)

PARTICIPANTS
(APA, 2010, pp. 29-30;
Creswell, 2008, pp. 150-159, 212-220)

INSTRUMENTS AND MATERIALS
(APA, 2010, p. 31;
Creswell, 2008, pp. 167-178, 220-232)

DESIGN AND PROCEDURE: Follows the instruments and materials section with a new, indented paragraph under the left-justified, boldface heading.

FINDINGS: A new, indented paragraph that begins immediately after the design and procedure section under the centered, boldface heading.

Design and Procedure

This mixed-method action research project employed a cross-sectional survey and semi-structured interview to address the primary questions of interest. All participants ($N = 94$) completed the survey instrument, and a sub-sample ($n = 10$) completed the semi-structured interview. Multiple data points (i.e., surveys and interviews) with community stakeholders (i.e., parents, teachers, and parishioners) were used to triangulate and validate the data.

An announcement explaining this action research project appeared in the parish bulletin and school newsletter in September 2010, two weeks after a series of town hall meetings to discuss the proposed consolidation of several local Catholic schools. Interested participants provided their contact information and were mailed a consent form (see Appendix C) and a paper survey to complete at their convenience. Completed surveys and consent forms were returned to the researcher in a self-addressed, stamped envelope. The same sample of participants was contacted independent of the request to complete the survey to participate in an individual interview with the researcher. Interviews were conducted at Saint Michael School in the researcher's office. Interviews were audio recorded and typically lasted between 30 to 45 minutes. Survey and interview data collection was completed by December 2010.

In addition to the survey and interview data, the researcher collected school enrollment data for the past 5 years. This data was used to establish a general trajectory of enrollment trends at Saint Michael School and to address concerns about declining enrollment that were expressed in the survey and interviews.

Findings

The purpose of this action research project was to examine factors that impact the accessibility and affordability of a Saint Michael education, and explore stakeholder perceptions of the proposed consolidation plan. An original survey instrument and semi-structured interviews were used in this mixed-method study. An analysis of variance (ANOVA) was used to analyze

---

DESIGN AND PROCEDURE (APA, 2010, pp. 31-32; Creswell, 2008, pp. 55-56, 59-63)

FINDINGS (APA, 2010, pp. 32-35; Creswell, 2008, pp. 56-59, 182-211, 243-270)

the quantitative survey data and open coding techniques were used to identify emergent themes in the semi-structured interview data. Additionally, a basic descriptive analysis was conducted on enrollment data for the past 5 years.

Inferential statistics were used to examine stakeholder responses to four questions on the survey instrument. The ANOVA revealed significant differences among the key stakeholder groups for three of the questions of interest: Important Ministry $F(3,90) = 22.94$, $p < .01$, Parish/School Connection $F(3,90) = 28.83$, $p < .01$, and Resources $F(3,90) = 5.59$, $p < .01$ (see Table 1).

Post hoc comparisons of stakeholder groups within each question revealed the nature of these general between group differences. When asked to indicate their agreement with the statement that Saint Michael School is an important ministry of Saint Michael Parish, parishioner-parents ($M = 3.50$, $SD = 0.51$) and teachers ($M = 3.67$, $SD = 0.57$) indicated significantly higher agreement than both non-parishioner-parents ($M = 2.59$, $SD = 0.76$) and parishioner-non-parents ($M = 2.44$, $SD = 0.49$).... [section continues].

Next, a correlation analysis was conducted to determine the relationship between number of years affiliated with the parish or school and agreement with importance of the ministry of Saint Michael School for the parish (see Table 2). The correlation revealed a significant negative correlation between these variables of interest, $r(94) = -0.35$, $p < .01$. This finding indicates that as years of affiliation increase, agreement with the valuing the ministry of the school decreases. Qualitative data collected from the final three questions of the interview protocol were analyzed using constant comparative coding to complement the primary quantitative analyses. The final questions in the interview protocol asked participants to share their thoughts on the impact of the consolidation, their personal concerns, and any other general thoughts or comments they would like to share. Analysis of the data provided through these questions revealed three major themes: parish-school connection, academic and extracurricular opportunities, and finances.

The most frequent response to the interview questions related to the parish-school

DISCUSSION AND EXTENSION: A new indented paragraph that begins immediately after the findings section under the centered, capitalized, boldface heading.

connection (57 text segments). Nearly all participants articulated a sense of loss of an important connection between the parish and the school. A teacher captured this general sentiment when she stated, "Saint Michael School has a great relationship with the parish. I am afraid that this new [consolidated] school will lose the important connection to the parish community." A parent echoed this concern, stating that "[My child] has found a real community here at Saint Michael School. She sees her friends at school during the week and at Mass [and other church functions] on the weekend…this is a special connection that will be lost when the schools combine." These parent and teacher comments reflect a concern that consolidating schools will compromise the important connection between the life of the parish and the school.... [section continues].

Finally, a brief descriptive analysis was conducted on the enrollment data for the past five years at Saint Michael Parish (see Figure 1). Over the past 5 years, enrollment at Saint Michael School has decreased by 11% ($N = 17$). While there was a slight increase in student enrollment from 2006 to 2008, there has been a general downward trend for the past 5 years.

The data from this mixed-method action research project reveal important differences in stakeholder perceptions regarding the proposed consolidation of Saint Michael School. Stakeholders are concerned that the proposed consolidation will compromise or diminish the important parish school connection, but also recognize that there are important benefits to be had in academic and extracurricular activities by consolidating schools. The implication of these findings will be discussed in the following section.

Discussion and Extension

The purpose of this action research project was to explore stakeholder perceptions of the proposed school consolidation plan. An original survey instrument and semi-structured interviews were used in this mixed-method study. The primary analysis of data indicated significant differences among stakeholders' perceptions of the proposed consolidation of Saint Michael School.

DISCUSSION AND EXTENSION (APA, 2010, pp. 35-36; Creswell, 2008, pp. 207-208, 264-266)

PERSPECTIVES ON CATHOLIC SCHOOL CONSOLIDATION   10

Discussion of Major Findings

     As expected, the descriptive analysis of enrollment data revealed a general decline in enrollment over the past five years (11% overall). The decline in enrollment does not represent a large number (only 17 students), nor is it as drastic as other schools in the area (i.e., Saint Stanislaus and Sacred Heart enrollments have declined 25% and 27% respectively over the same time period). However, with multiple Catholic schools in the urban core experiencing similar trends, action steps must be taken to remediate this marked decline (McDonald & Schultz, 2010). Consolidation is one such option to address the overall issue of declining enrollment in urban Catholic schools across the country. Yet, there are some concerns among key stakeholder groups about the impact of school consolidation on the parish and school community. Parishioner-parents and teachers—stakeholders with distinct personal and professional connections to the parish and school—indicated the highest agreement with the importance of Saint Michael School to the parish. Said another way, individuals with the greatest personal and professional investment in the school were more likely to see its value to the overall ministry of the parish. Furthermore, these same stakeholders were concerned that consolidation will abrogate the important and life-giving relationship that currently exists between the parish and the school.

     However, school consolidation is not without benefits. Increasing enrollment through consolidation would provide additional income to the school that could be used to expand academic programs and extracurricular activities. These economies of scale provide financial advantages that, properly managed, can have positive impact on the educational opportunities at the school (Ash, 2007; Dodson & Garrett, 2004). Participants who were interviewed for this study acknowledged these potential benefits—yet, some seemed hesitant to admit that the benefits of consolidation could outweigh the cost to the parish and school community.

Application of Findings

     This action research project has revealed that there are strong and varied opinions on the proposed consolidation of St Michael Catholic School. These stakeholder opinions provide valuable insight into the perceived importance and viability of Catholic education in this community. Therefore, it is my recommendation that this study should be replicated in all school and parish communities affected by the proposed plan for consolidation. Once the school- and parish-based replication has been completed, town-hall style meetings and listening sessions can be held to engage and inform all school stakeholders. This systematic and comprehensive approach to seeking information from persons interested and invested in local Catholic education will ensure that the personnel responsible for recommending school closure and consolidation will have the most accurate, reliable, and representative data to inform their decisions.

In addition to providing important information regarding the proposed consolidation of local Catholic schools, this action research project highlighted a concerning disparity in stakeholders' perception of the value of the school to the overall ministry of the parish. While the cause of this disparity is unclear (e.g., no children in the parish school, concern over the financial impact of the school on other parish ministries, etc.), school and parish personnel must redouble their efforts to inform all parishioners that the high quality, faith-filled education provided at St. Michael school is integral to the overall educative mission of the Church. Parishioner understanding and support of a robust education in the faith through our Catholic schools is essential to the long-term viability of Catholic education in this community, regardless of what happens with the proposed consolidation.

Dissemination

The results and final research report of this AR project will be shared with the pastor of Saint Michael Parish and the Saint Michael School Board at their spring meeting in May 2011. A five-page research brief will also be prepared for dissemination among study participants and used in town-hall style meetings with other key stakeholders as the principal and school board members continue to investigate the potential impact of school consolidation on Saint Michael

Parish and School.

Limitations

A limitation of the study arose from the sampling technique used to solicit participants for the study. An announcement of the study was printed in the parish bulletin and school newsletter; anyone interested in the study was asked to participate. This convenience sample may not accurately represent all stakeholder groups since individuals with strong feelings or interest in the issue of consolidation could have been more motivated to respond. The fact that 86% of teachers (12 out of 14) responded to the open invitation speaks to this limitation—no other group had such a high response rate or such a tangible professional investment in the issue of consolidation. This limitation could be mitigated in future studies by identifying stakeholders from parish and school rosters rather than relying solely on the personal interest and initiative of participants.

Future Directions

Designing and implementing this study with key stakeholders in the parish and school community has been an insightful and rewarding process. Asking participants to share their thoughts and feelings on an issue so central to my professional responsibilities and so integral to the parish community has inspired this researcher to collaborate with other principals of schools targeted for this consolidation. Beginning in September 2011, this researcher will work with two other principals to design an AR project that addresses the same research questions in two other parishes in the urban core. These results will then be compared to the data collected in this AR project at Saint Michael Parish and School.

For nearly 200 years the parish school has served as the "privileged environment in which Christian education is carried out" (Congregation for Catholic Education, 1998, para. 11). Seen through this lens, the parish school is a vital and vibrant component of parish life wherein the young receive an education inspired by Christ and nurtured through a distinct and tangible connection to the larger Church. The proposed consolidation of Saint Michael School is about more than moving buildings or changing the governance model of an organization—it speaks to the fundamental importance of Christian education to the overall life and ministry of the parish.

REFERENCES: Follow the discussion and extension section and begin on a new page under the centered, capitalized heading. First line of each reference is NOT indented, but the following lines in each citation are indented (use the ruler to create the hanging indent). Double-space within and between references.

PERSPECTIVES ON CATHOLIC SCHOOL CONSOLIDATION   14

References

REFERENCES (APA, 2010, p. 37)

Ash, K. (2007, December 24). In consolidating districts, states run tricky course to secure local

support. *Education Week, 27*(9), 22-23. Retrieved from http://www.edweek.org

Brinig, M. F., & Garnett, N. S. (2010). Catholic schools, urban neighborhoods, and education

reform. *Notre Dame Law Review, 85*(3), 887-954. Retrieved from http://papers.ssrn.com

Congregation for Catholic Education. (1998). *The Catholic school on the threshold of the third*

millennium. Boston: Pauline Books and Media.

Dodson, M. E., & Garrett, T. A. (2004). Inefficient education spending in public school districts:

A case for consolidation? *Contemporary Economic Policy, 22*(2), 270-280. doi:10.1093/

cep/byh019

Golway, T. (2007, December 10). A future without parish schools. *America,* p. 8. Retrieved from

http://www.americamagazine.org

Green, E. (2011, January 19). Study explores economic benefits of Catholic education [Web log

post]. Retrieved from http://weblogs.baltimoresun.com/news/education/blog/2011/01/

benefits_of_catholic_education.html

Hamilton, S. W. (Ed.). (2008). *Who will save America's urban Catholic schools?* Washington,

DC: Thomas B. Fordham Institute.

Kileen, K., & Sipple, J. (2000). *School consolidation and transportation policy: An empirical*

and institutional analysis. Retrieved from http://www.ruraledu.org/articles.php?id=2047

Lee, V. E., & Loeb, S. (2000). School size in Chicago elementary schools: Effects on teach-

ers' attitudes and students' achievement. *Education Research Journal, 37*(1), 3-31.

doi:10.3102/00028312037001003

Lee, V. E., & Smith, J. B. (1997). High school size: Which works best for whom? *Educational*

Evaluation and Policy Analysis, 19(3), 205-227. doi:10.3012/01623737019003205

McCluskey, N. G. (Ed.). (1964). *Catholic education in America: A documented history.* New

PERSPECTIVES ON CATHOLIC SCHOOL CONSOLIDATION   15

York: Columbia.

McDonald, D., & Shultz, M. (2010). *The annual statistical report on schools, enrollment, and
    staffing*. Arlington, VA: National Catholic Educational Association.

McLaughlin, T., O'Keefe, J., & O'Keeffe, B. (Eds.). (1996). *The contemporary Catholic school:
    Context, identity, and diversity*. London: Routledge.

National Center for Education Statistics (2010). *Digest of education statistics: 2009*. Retrieved
    from http://www.nces.ed.gov

Walch, T. (2003). *Parish school: American Catholic parochial education from colonial times to
    the present*. Washington, DC: National Catholic Educational Association.

PERSPECTIVES ON CATHOLIC SCHOOL CONSOLIDATION   16

Table 1

Mean, Standard Deviation, and ANOVA for Stakeholder Responses to School Survey

Variable	Parishioner Parent ($n = 30$)		Non-Parishioner Parent ($n = 27$)		Parishioner Non-Parent ($n = 25$)		Saint Michael Teacher ($n = 12$)		ANOVA
	M	*SD*	*M*	*SD*	*M*	*SD*	*M*	*SD*	*F* (3,90)
School is an important ministry of the parish	3.50	0.51	2.59	0.57	2.44	0.76	3.67	0.49	22.94*
Strong connection between parish and school	3.43	0.68	2.44	0.51	2.16	0.68	3.58	0.85	28.83*
Consolidation will be beneficial for the parish	2.40	1.10	2.48	1.25	2.72	1.06	2.25	1.29	0.59
Sufficient resources without consolidation	2.37	0.49	1.93	0.67	1.80	0.65	2.33	0.14	5.59*
Consolidation will improve the quality of Catholic education	1.80	0.65	1.67	0.48	1.96	0.73	1.42	0.51	2.33

Note. * $p < .01$

Table 2

Correlation Coefficients for Years Affiliated with Parish and Importance of Saint Michael School to the Parish

Variable	1	2
1. Number of years affiliated with the parish/school	--	-0.35*
2. Importance of Saint Michael School to the parish	-0.35*	--

Note. * $p < .01$

PERSPECTIVES ON CATHOLIC SCHOOL CONSOLIDATION   18

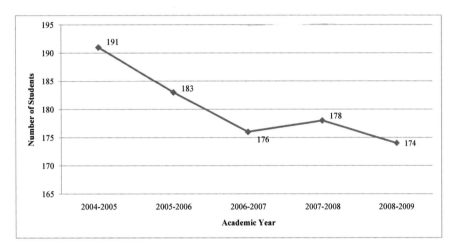

Figure 1. Enrollment trend at Saint Michael School from 2004-2009

PERSPECTIVES ON CATHOLIC SCHOOL CONSOLIDATION   19

Appendix A

Sample Survey Protocol

School Perceptions Survey – Saint Michael Parish and School

Dear Stakeholder,
Please answer the following questions to the best of your ability. Remember, there are no right or wrong answers and your responses are completely anonymous.

Affiliation with Saint Michael Parish and/or School (circle one):

| *Parishioner and parent of current Saint Michael Student* | *Non-parishioner and parent of current Saint Michael Student* | *Parishioner without school-age children* | *Teacher at Saint Michael School* |

Number of years affiliated in this capacity: _____

Please respond to the following questions by selecting the answer that is best for you; there are no right or wrong answers. Remember that your answers are anonymous and will only be reported as group averages.

1. Saint Michael School is an important ministry of Saint Michael Parish.

   Strongly Disagree   *Disagree*   *Agree*   *Strongly Agree*

2. There is a strong connection between Saint Michael Parish and School.

   Strongly Disagree   *Disagree*   *Agree*   *Strongly Agree*

3. The proposed school consolidation will be beneficial for Saint Michael Parish.

   Strongly Disagree   *Disagree*   *Agree*   *Strongly Agree*

4. Saint Michael School has sufficient resources to meet the needs of its students without consolidating.

   Strongly Disagree   *Disagree*   *Agree*   *Strongly Agree*

5. The proposed school consolidation will improve the quality of Catholic education in our community.

   Strongly Disagree   *Disagree*   *Agree*   *Strongly Agree*

General Comments:

PERSPECTIVES ON CATHOLIC SCHOOL CONSOLIDATION   20

Appendix B

Sample Semi-Structured Interview Protocol

Date of Interview:

Time of Interview:

Location of Interview:

Participant Name:

Participant Position/Occupation:

1. Please describe your affiliation or connection with Saint Michael School and/or parish. How many years have you had this affiliation or connection?

2. Can you tell me what you know about the proposed school consolidation? How did you find out about it?

3. How do you think the proposed school consolidation will impact the Saint Michael School and Parish community?

4. What is your biggest concern regarding the proposed consolidation?

5. Do you have any other general thoughts or comments you would like to share?

Appendix C

Sample Consent Form

 Saint Michael Catholic School

Dear School Partner,

Thank you for your interest in participating in this study examining perceptions and issues regarding the proposed consolidation of Saint Michael Catholic School. We hope to learn what factors impact student enrollment at Saint Michael Catholic School and perceptions of the proposed consolidation with another local Catholic school. You have been selected to participate because you are a stakeholder in the parish and school community and responded to the announcement in the parish bulletin or school newsletter.

If you decide to participate in this study, you will receive a paper survey in the mail. The survey contains both multiple choice and open response questions regarding your perceptions of the proposed school consolidation. The survey should take no more that 25 minutes to complete. I do not foresee any risks to you for participating in the study. You participation could yield benefits by providing insight into the important issues facing our school community. Additionally, you will be contacted independent of the survey to participate in an interview with the researcher.

Your participation in this study is entirely voluntary; you are free to refuse to participate or to withdraw your consent to participate in this research at any time without penalty or prejudice. Your privacy will be protected because you will not be identified by name as a participant in this project. Data from the survey will be reported only in aggregate form and your responses will not be identified individually.

If you have any questions about the study or your participation, please contact me at the information below. I would like to thank you in advance for your time and consideration.

Sincerely,

Mrs. Theresa Q. Principal
principal@stmichael.org
222-333-4444

You are making a decision to participate in the study described above. Your signature indicates that you are at least 18 years old, have read the information in the above letter, and have decided to participate in the study.

Participant Name (please print)   Date

Participant Signature

References

Action Research Journal. (2011, January 24). Mission statement [Web page]. Retrieved from http://arj.sagepub.com/

Alokolaro, A. O. (2008). Critical consumers of information in the language arts. In J. M. Frabutt, A. C. Holter, & R. J. Nuzzi (Eds.), *Research, action, and change: Leaders reshaping Catholic schools* (pp. 91-118). Notre Dame, IN: Alliance for Catholic Education Press.

American Psychological Association. (2005). *Concise rules of APA style*. Washington, DC: Author.

American Psychological Association. (2010). *Publication manual of the American Psychological Association* (6th ed.). Washington, DC: Author.

Anderson, G. L., Herr, K., & Nihlen, A. S. (1994). *Studying your own school: An educator's guide to qualitative practitioner research*. Thousand Oaks, CA: Corwin Press.

Asmar, K. M. (2008a, November). *The effect of an English language acquisition program on the academic literacy, English fluency, and reading achievement of second grade ELL students.* Paper presented at the Association for Moral Education 34th Annual Conference, Notre Dame, IN.

Asmar, K. M. (2008b). The effect of an English language acquisition program on the academic literacy, English fluency, and reading achievement of second grade ELL students. In J. M. Frabutt, A. C. Holter, & R. J. Nuzzi (Eds.), *Research, action, and change: Leaders reshaping Catholic schools* (pp. 119-133). Notre Dame, IN: Alliance for Catholic Education Press.

Bayer, D. (2008). *Exploring the impact of the one-to-one laptop program at St. Joachim School.* Unpublished manuscript, University of Notre Dame.

Benedict XVI. (2008). *Address to educators.* Retrieved April 3, 2009, from http://www. uspapalvisit.org

Bickman, L., Rog, D. J., & Hedrick, T. E. (1998). Applied research design: A practical approach. In L. Bickman & D. J. Rog (Eds.), *Handbook of applied social science research methods* (pp. 5-38). Thousand Oaks, CA: Sage.

Borg, W. R., & Gall, M. (1989). *Educational research: An introduction* (5th ed.). New York: Longman.

Burleigh, A. C. (2009). *Assessing the current relationship between St. Mary Parish and School.* Unpublished manuscript, University of Notre Dame.

Catholic Education: A Journal of Inquiry and Practice. (2011, January 24). Mission statement [Web page]. Retrieved from http://ejournals.bc.edu/ojs/index.php/catholic

Cochran-Smith, M., & Lytle, S. L. (1999). The teacher research movement a decade later. *Educational Researcher, 28*(7), 15-25. doi:10.3102/0013189X028007015

Cohen, J. (1988). *Statistical power analysis for the behavioral sciences* (2nd ed.). Hillsdale, NJ: Academic Press.

Cohen, J. (1992). A power primer. *Psychological Bulletin, 112*(1), 155-159. doi:10.1037/0033-2909.112.1.155

Congregation for Catholic Education. (1998). *The Catholic school on the threshold of the third millennium.* Boston: Pauline Books and Media.

Cortina, J. M. (1993). What is a coefficient alpha? An examination of theory and applications. *Journal of Applied Psychology, 78,* 98-104. doi:10.1037/0021-9010.78.1.98

Creswell, J. (2006). *Qualitative inquiry and research design: Choosing among five approaches* (2nd ed.). Thousand Oaks, CA: Sage.

Creswell, J. W. (2008). *Educational research: Planning, conducting, and evaluating quantitative and qualitative research* (3rd ed.). Upper Saddle River, NJ: Pearson Education.

Cronbach, L. J. (1951). Coefficient alpha and internal structure of tests. *Psychometrika, 16,* 297-334. doi:10.1007/BF02310555

Dana, N. F., & Yendol-Silva, D. (2003). *The reflective educator's guide to classroom research.* Thousand Oaks, CA: Corwin Press.

Duncan, A. G. (2008, July). *Effects of ability grouping for literacy instruction in kindergarten.* Poster session presented at the ACE Leadership 1st Annual Conference, Notre Dame, IN.

Educational Action Research. (2011, January 24). Mission statement [Web page]. Retrieved from http://www.tandf.co.uk/journals/titles/09650792.asp

Eisenhart, M. (2006). Representing qualitative data. In J. L. Green, G. Camilli, P. B. Elmore, A. Skukauskaitė, & E. Grace (Eds.), *Handbook of complementary methods in education research* (pp. 567-581). Mahwah, NJ: Lawrence Erlbaum.

Field, A. (2009). *Discovering statistics using SPSS* (3rd ed.). Thousand Oaks, CA: Sage.

Fierro, M. (2008, November). *Learning to read, reading to learn.* Paper presented at the Association for Moral Education 34th Annual Conference, Notre Dame, IN.

Fowler, F. J. (1998). Design and evaluation of survey questions. In L. Bickman & D. J. Rog (Eds.), *Handbook of applied social science research methods* (pp. 343-376). Thousand Oaks, CA: Sage.

Fowler, F. J. (2009). *Survey research methods* (4th ed.). Thousand Oaks, CA: Sage.

Frabutt, J. M., Holter, A. C., & Nuzzi, R. J. (2008). *Research, action, and change: Leaders reshaping Catholic schools.* Notre Dame, IN: Alliance for Catholic Education Press.

Frazier, D. S. (2008). IDEA services for Catholic school children with disabilities in the Diocese of Jefferson City. In J. M. Frabutt, A. C. Holter, & R. J. Nuzzi (Eds.), *Research, action, and change: Leaders reshaping Catholic schools* (pp. 67-90). Notre Dame, IN: Alliance for Catholic Education Press.

Friese, B., & Bogenschneider, K. (2009). The voice of experience: How social scientists communicate family research to policy makers. *Family Relations, 58,* 229-243.

Gaventa, J., & Cornwall, A. (2001). Power and knowledge. In P. Reason & H. Bradbury (Eds.), *Handbook of action research: Participative inquiry and practice* (pp. 70-80). London: Sage.

Gay, L. R., Mills, G. E., & Airasian, P. (2009). *Educational research: Competencies for analysis and applications* (9th ed.). London: Pearson Education.

Grayson, D. (2004). Some myths and legends in quantitative psychology. *Understanding Statistics, 3*(1), 101-134. doi:10.1207/S15328031US0302_3

Hammack, F. M. (1997). Ethical issues in teacher research. *Teachers College Record, 99*(2), 247-265. Retrieved from http://www.tcrecord.org/

Hanson, D. M. (2007). Crossing bridges of culture, color, and language. In C. Caro-Bruce, R. Flessner, M. Klehr, & K. Zeichner (Eds.), *Creating equitable classrooms through action research* (pp. 254-274). Thousand Oaks, CA: Corwin Press.

Healy, C. A. (2008). Student literacy experiences at La Salle Catholic College Preparatory in Milwaukie, Oregon. In J. M. Frabutt, A. C. Holter, & R. J. Nuzzi (Eds.), *Research, action, and change: Leaders reshaping Catholic schools* (pp. 179-220). Notre Dame, IN: Alliance for Catholic Education Press.

Hendricks, C. (2006). *Improving schools through action research: A comprehensive guide for educators.* Boston: Pearson.

Henry, G. T. (1990). *Practical sampling.* Newbury Park, CA: Sage.

Henry, G. T. (1998). Practical sampling. In L. Bickman & D. J. Rog (Eds.), *Handbook of applied social science research methods* (pp. 101-126). Thousand Oaks, CA: Sage.

Hobson, D. (2001). Learning with each other: Collaboration in teacher research. In G. Burnaford, J. Fischer, & D. Hobson (Eds.), *Teachers doing research: The power of action through inquiry* (2nd ed., pp. 173-191). Mahwah, NJ: Lawrence Erlbaum.

Holly, M. L., Arhar, J. M., & Kasten, W. C. (2009). *Action research for teachers: Traveling the yellow brick road* (3rd ed.). Boston: Pearson Education.

Hui, M. F. (2008). Cultivating creativity in the classroom: Assessment strategies to improve teaching and learning. In M. F. Hui & D. L. Grossman (Eds.), *Improving teacher education through action research* (pp. 42-59). New York: Routledge.

Hui, M. F., & Grossman, D. L. (Eds.). (2008). *Improving teacher education through action research.* New York: Routledge.

i.e.: inquiry in education. (2011, June 2). Journal home [Web page]. Retrieved from http://digitalcommons.nl.edu/ie/

Individuals with Disabilities Education Improvement Act, 20 U.S.C. §1401 *et seq.* (2004).

Izumi, B. T., Schultz, A. J., Israel, B. A., Reyes, A. G., Martin, J., Lichtenstein, R. L., Wilson, C., & Sand, S. L. (2010). The one-pager: A practical policy advocacy tool for translating community-based participatory research into action. *Progress in Community Health Partnerships: Research, Education, and Action, 4*(2), 141-147.

James, E. A., Milenkiewicz, M. T., & Bucknam, A. (2008). *Participatory action research for educational leadership: Using data-driven decision making to improve schools.* Thousand Oaks, CA: Sage.

Johnson, A. P. (2008). *A short guide to action research.* Boston: Pearson.

Johnson, B., & Christensen, L. (2004). *Educational research: Quantitative, qualitative, and mixed method approaches* (2nd ed.). Boston: Pearson Education.

Kline, P. (1999). *The handbook of psychological testing* (2nd ed.). New York: Routledge.

Kmack, S. (2008). The effects of an advisory program for at-risk first year high school students. In J. M. Frabutt, A. C. Holter, & R. J. Nuzzi (Eds.), *Research, action, and change: Leaders reshaping Catholic schools* (pp. 135-177). Notre Dame, IN: Alliance for Catholic Education Press.

Levinson, P. (Ed.). (1982). *In pursuit of truth: Essays on the philosophy of Carl Popper on the occasion of his 80th birthday.* Atlantic Highlands, NJ: Humanities Press.

Lipsey, M. W. (1990). *Design sensitivity: Statistical power for experimental research.* Newbury Park, CA: Sage.

Locke, L. F., Silverman, S. J., & Spirduso, W. W. (2004). *Reading and understanding research* (2nd ed.). Thousand Oaks, CA: Sage.

McCann-Ojeda, K. (2008, July). *Parishioner enrollment in and support of St. Michael the Archangel Catholic School in Silver Spring, Maryland.* Poster session presented at the ACE Leadership 1st Annual Conference, Notre Dame, IN.

McLellan, E., MacQueen, K. M., & Neidig, J. L. (2003). Beyond the qualitative interview: Data preparation and transcription. *Field Methods, 15*(1), 63-84. doi:10.1177/1525822X02239573

Mertens, D. M. (1998). *Research methods in education and psychology.* Thousand Oaks, CA: Sage.

Mertler, C. A. (2009). *Action research: Teachers as researchers in the classroom* (2nd ed.). Thousand Oaks, CA: Sage.

Mertler, C. A., & Charles, C. M. (2008). *Introduction to educational research* (6th ed.). Boston: Pearson.

Miller, J. M. (2006). *The Holy See's teaching on Catholic schools.* Atlanta, GA: Solidarity Association.

Mohr, M., Rogers, C., Sanford, B., Nocerino, M. A., MacLean, M. S., & Clawson, S. (Eds). (2004). *Teacher research for better schools.* New York: Teachers College Press.

Moore, L. P. (2004). Community. In T. C. Hunt, E. A. Joseph, & R. J. Nuzzi (Eds.), *Catholic schools in the United States: An encyclopedia* (Vol. 1, pp. 172-174). Westport, CT: Greenwood Press.

National Commission for the Protection of Human Subjects of Biomedical and Behavioral Research. (1979). *The Belmont report: Ethical principles and guidelines for the protection of human subjects of biomedical and behavioral research.* Retrieved November 7, 2008, from http://www.hhs.gov/ohrp/humansubjects/guidance/belmont.htm

Ng, E. M. (2008). Using IT to foster cooperative learning and peer assessment. In M. F. Hui & D. L. Grossman (Eds.), *Improving teacher education through action research* (pp. 99-114). New York: Routledge.

Nicol, A. A. M., & Pexman, P. M. (1999). *Presenting your findings: A practical guide for creating tables.* Washington, DC: American Psychological Association.

Nolen, A., & Vander Putten, J. (2007). Action research in education: Addressing gaps in ethical principles and practices. *Educational Researcher, 36,* 401-407. doi:10.3102/0013189X07309629

O'Linn, F. W., & Scott, M. E. (2008). Evaluating the impact of the St. Edward High School pre-engineering program on successful collegiate engineering study. In J. M. Frabutt, A. C. Holter, & R. J. Nuzzi (Eds.), *Research, action, and change: Leaders reshaping Catholic schools* (pp. 239-259). Notre Dame, IN: Alliance for Catholic Education Press.

Pierre-Antoine, J. (2008, July). *In mission together to praise, bless, and preach: Fostering the charism of the Dominican Sisters of Mission San Jose at St. Edward Parish School.* Poster session presented at the ACE Leadership 1st Annual Conference, Notre Dame, IN.

Pritchard, I. (2002). Travelers and trolls: Practitioner research and institutional review boards. *Educational Researcher, 31,* 3-13. doi:10.3102/0013189X031003003

Rearick, M. L., & Feldman, A. (1999). Orientations, purposes, and reflection: A framework for understanding action research. *Teaching and Teacher Education, 15,* 333-349. doi:10.1016/S0742-051X(98)00053-5

Richards, S. (2007). What strategies can I incorporate so that the English language learners in my classroom will better understand oral directions? In C. Caro-Bruce, R. Flessner, M. Klehr, & K. Zeichner (Eds.), *Creating equitable classrooms through action research* (pp. 59-77). Thousand Oaks, CA: Corwin Press.

Robinson, V., & Lai, M. K. (2006). *Practitioner research for educators: A guide to improving classrooms and schools.* Thousand Oaks, CA: Corwin Press.

Sacred Congregation for Catholic Education. (1982). *Lay Catholics in schools: Witnesses to faith.* Boston: St. Paul.

Sanford, B. (2004). It all adds up: Learning number facts in first grade. In M. M. Mohr, C. Rogers, B. Sanford, M. A. Nocerino, M. S. MacLean, & S. Clawson (Eds.), *Teacher research for better schools* (pp. 38-48). New York: Teachers College Press.

Sagor, R. (2005). *The action research guidebook: A four-step process for educators and school teams.* Thousand Oaks, CA: Corwin Press.

Shadish, W. R., Cook, T. D., & Campbell, D. T. (2002). *Experimental and quasi-experimental designs for generalized causal inference.* Boston: Houghton Mifflin.

Somekh, B. (2006). *Action research: A methodology for change and development.* Maidenhead, Berkshire, UK: Open University Press.

Stocking, S. H., & Sparks, J. V. (2007). Communicating the complexities of and uncertainties of behavioral science. In M. K. Welch-Ross & L. G. Fasig (Eds.), *Handbook on communicating and disseminating behavioral science* (pp. 73-92). Thousand Oaks, CA: Sage.

Strauss, A., & Corbin, J. (1998). *Basics of qualitative research* (2nd ed.). Thousand Oaks, CA: Sage.

Strauss, A. L., & Corbin, J. M. (1998). *Basics of qualitative data: Techniques and procedures for developing grounded inquiry* (2nd ed.). Thousand Oaks, CA: Sage.

Stringer, E. T. (2007). *Action research* (3rd ed.). Thousand Oaks, CA: Sage.

Suter, W. N. (2006). *Introduction to educational research: A critical thinking approach.* Thousand Oaks, CA: Sage.

Thomas, R. M. (2005). *Teachers doing research: An introductory guidebook.* Boston: Pearson Education.

Thompson, K. T. (2009). *The impact of block scheduling on middle school math achievement.* Unpublished manuscript, University of Notre Dame.

United States Conference of Catholic Bishops. (2005). *Renewing our commitment to Catholic elementary and secondary schools in the third millennium.* Washington, DC: Author.

Vatican Council II. (1965). *Gravissimum educationis* [Declaration on Christian education]. Rome: Libreria Editrice Vaticana.

Virginia Adult Education Research Network. (2000). *Sample criteria for writing research briefs.* Retrieved from http://www.valrc.org/publications/research/meetings/meeting4/session13/index.html

Wamba, N. G. (2006). Action research in school leadership programs. *Academic Exchange Quarterly, 10*(2), 51-56. Retrieved from http://www.rapidintellect.com/AEQweb

World Medical Association. (1964). *World Medical Association Declaration of Helsinki. Ethical principles for medical research involving human subjects* (last amended October 2008). Retrieved November 7, 2008, from http://www.wma.net/e/policy/b3.htm

Zeichner, K. (2001). Educational action research. In P. Reason & H. Bradbury (Eds.), *Handbook of action research: Participative inquiry and practice* (pp. 273-283). Thousand Oaks, CA: Sage.

Appendix A :
Sample Interview Transcripts
and Qualitative Coding

Saint Michael School Consolidation Study

Contents:

The authors acknowledge Ms. Amy Grinsteinner of the University of Notre Dame, who contributed significantly to the development of this section while serving as an undergraduate research assistant for the Mary Ann Remick Leadership Program.

1

Date of Interview: 26 October 2008
Time of Interview: 10:00 A.M.
Location of Interview: Saint Michael School
Participant Name: Miguel Gonzalez
Participant Position/Occupation: Accountant

Interviewer: Alright, so to begin today can you tell me about your connection with Saint Michael School and Parish?

Parishioner/Parent: Sure. My daughter Maria is a sixth grader at Saint Michael. As for me, I've been a member of Saint Michael Parish for the past 9 years. Oh, and I'm also on the Parish Finance Committee. Been doing that for, wow, must be 6 years now.

I: Ok, excellent. So, to get to the heart of the matter, can you tell me what you know about the proposed consolidation?

PP: Sure. So Saint Michael is having trouble keeping enrollment numbers up. The finances…let's just say they are losing money faster than they can bring it in. So, uh, in attempt to get these problems fixed the school board came up with this, this idea that we combine our school with three other Catholic schools, that we consolidate. From what I hear, their idea is to put everybody together in this brand new building that they want to build, uh, that's about 3 miles away from the church.

I: And how did you find this out?

PP: Our pastor told me one day after a Finance Committee meeting.

I: Well, I'd say that's a pretty reliable source. (Laughter) And now, do you think this consolidation would have an effect on the Saint Michael School and Parish, and uh, if so, how?

PP: I think the new school would completely change the school and parish community, uh, as it exists today. Do I think that this change has to be bad thing? I would say, um, not necessarily. On the one hand, there are, I talk to a lot of parishioners who experience, um, a—a sense of ownership of the school and they, uh, take pride in it. If the school went from "Saint Michael" to "Four Different Parishes in the Community" I guess some of these people might lose that, uh, those ties to the school. That's, uh, that's one of the negative ways I look at it. Another negative is how it might affect the kids. I mean, Maria has found a real community here at Saint Michael School. She sees her friends at school during the week and at Mass on the weekend. Also, um, these kids are all in youth group together. The group sometimes has weekend service projects or takes fields trips or other things. This is a special connection that will be lost when the schools combine. But, uh, like I said before, I don't really think these changes will end badly. I mean, the kids will still be in church on the weekends and still be active with the youth group, so the, the other parishioners will still see them and have a, I guess a good relationship with them. And the kids will still be in these weekend groups and they will all make the switch together, so it's not like combining would, uh, have to tear friendships apart or anything like that.

I: Right. That takes us to my next question—what is your biggest concern about this proposal?

PP: Well, my number one concern is of course always for my child. Maria is at a, um, tender time in her life right now. You know, she's just beginning to find out for herself who she is as a person. If the plan goes through, there's, uh, there's going to be a major shake-up in her life. Even though all her friends would move with her, she would still be, be surrounded by unfamiliar faces and places. Then there is also the concern about her personal safety. Now, I'm not saying I think the kids at… at the other schools are bad kids. Not at all. What I'm saying is that I know Maria is safe at Saint Michael. I need to know that she is going to be safe and well taken care of at the new school. Another concern I feel that, uh, I need to talk about is finances. If, and before the board goes through with this plan, I just want to say that they need to come up with some sort of plan outlining what the parish contribution to the school would be. I mean, would each parish contribute the same amount to the school? Or, would each one just, um, just pay, like, based on percentage of students from their parish? So I'm also concerned about how this jump would affect the parish finances.

I: Alright, well that brings us to the end of my questions. Do you have any other thoughts or comments you would like to share before we close?

PP: (Chuckles) Yeah, I've got a lot of thoughts and comments on this topic that we haven't talked about yet. I know there are a lot of people out there who are feeling sort of negative about this plan. I gotta say, I've pretty much been a supporter since, well, since the day I heard about it. I think if we, if we don't go through with it we are shorting our kids on a good opportunity. I know what the money situation looks like at the school, I know it isn't good. And since we don't seem to, uh, to be expanding at a very quick rate, or at all, I think the consolidation is the best bet. Not only would we be not paying for a school that is, well, half full if even that, we would also be able to give our kids better resources in school and in, in extracurriculars. I mean, last year, Maria was using an English book that someone had signed in 1982. The school is using books that are, um, a generation old, but they can't replace them 'cause they don't have the money. Um, ok, here's another story for you: one of Maria's good friends Julia moved here a few years back. She'd been one of the best gymnasts at her school. Julia begged her parents to move her to a different school when, ah, when she found out Saint Michael couldn't support a gymnastics team. If we consolidate, we wouldn't even have these issues. We can't be thinking about the extra time it's going to take to drive to the new school. We can't be thinking that we won't know every person on the PTA. We gotta think about what's best for our kids. And, uh, I hate to say it, but right now Saint Michael's alone can't provide the best.

I: That's a good reason to be seriously looking at this proposal. Well, I don't have anything else for you today, and I know you need to be getting back to work, so I think that will do it for today. Thanks for taking the time to come in and chat with me.

PP: It was no problem. I'm pretty passionate about the consolidation, so anytime somebody wants to talk about it I jump at the chance.

I: Well that worked out for me then. (Laughter) Have a good day.

2

Date of Interview: 9 November 2010
Time of Interview: 12:00 P.M.
Location of Interview: Saint Michael School
Participant Name: Gabi Vasquez
Participant Position/Occupation: Fourth Grade Teacher, Saint Michael School

Interviewer: Ok, so to begin today, could you please describe your connection with Saint Michael School and the Parish?	
Teacher: Sure. I'm the **fourth grade teacher** at Saint Michael School, and I'm a **parishioner** at the parish.	-Affiliation: Teacher, Parishioner
I: And how long have you been in each of these roles?	
T: Well, I've been a **parishioner for six years and, um, I'm in my seventh year here at Saint Michael.** Uh, before I was, before coming to Saint Michael I taught for, um, four years at a Catholic school on the East Coast.	-Affiliation: 7 years
I: Great. So, as you know, I am interviewing you to get your, uh, your reaction to the proposed school consolidation. Can you tell me what you know about this plan?	
T: Um, what I know is that the school board is talking about **combining Saint Michael with the, uh, with three other Catholic schools** from the area. I guess they're talking about building a new school to hold all the kids from these, uh, different schools. This new school supposedly would be located down by, **located a few miles from the parish.**	-Knowledge about proposal: Combine with 3 schools, few miles away
I: Um, and how did you find out about this?	
T: **I found this out at the monthly faculty meeting** 'cause, uh, they gave a copy of the, the minutes from the school board meeting to us.	-Gained knowledge: faculty meeting
I: Ok. And now, um, how do you think this consolidation would impact the Saint Michael School and Parish community?	
T: Um, well I, I think the consolidation would have a huge impact on the community, and I don't know if…**I'm not sure that that impact would necessarily be a positive one.** You know, Saint Michael School has a great relationship with the	-Impact: Uncertain

parish. **I am afraid that this new school will lose the important connection to the parish community.** I mean, the school's not just gonna, um, house mainly kids from Saint Michael anymore, but there's gonna be students from a couple different parishes. And that gives, um…**I'm worried that this will lead to a loss of the, uh, the deep…the deep interconnectedness between the parish and the school.** And **I think the distance between the new school and the parish is also gonna hurt the community feeling.** With the school being so far away, it would probably, um, I think it would fall off a lot of our parishioners' radar screens and the only parishioners who would even be concerned about the school anymore would be parents of students.	-Loss of parish-school connection -Loss of parish-school connection -Concern: Distance
I: And so that leads into, what is your biggest concern about the proposal?	
T: Well, I've got several concerns about it. **The biggest is probably how it's going to affect the whole school/parish relationship,** but uh, I already talked about that before. **Another concern that I have, um, personally is about my own, about my teaching position.** I mean, would all the teachers from all the schools being combined get to keep their positions? And if the answer's no, how are they gonna decide who stays and who goes? I know I sound kinda, um, kinda selfish, but these are questions I gotta have answered before I could support the plan to combine, you know? Um, **another concern I have is about my students.** If the schools, um, if the schools go through with consolidation, my students are gonna have to leave the comfort of the school that they, that some have been attending for years and go to a place where their teachers, their classmates, and, uh, even the building are strange—unfamiliar to them. **I'm worried if the kids could handle that.**	-Loss of parish-school connection -Concern: Teaching position -Concern: Students' transition to new school -Concern: Students' transition to new school
I: Ok, well that covers all the formal questions I wanted to ask. Do you have any other thoughts you would like to share?	
T: Uh…yeah, I do. I'm sure that everything I've said so far to you makes it seem like I think that the consolidation is, um, the worst idea ever and could only have bad results for everyone that's, everyone involved. Really though, I don't think that. I know a lot of good could come from, uh, from consolidating. **One thing I'm really excited about is the funding we could get for more extracurricular stuff.** Right now, Saint Michael doesn't have enough money to be able to have a lot of extracurriculars that our students want to, to be in. But, at the new school, this wouldn't be the case.	-Benefit: Extracurriculars

I: Could you be more specific about what kinds of extracurriculars you are talking about? T: Well, ok, for example, when I first started at Saint Michael **I was the advisor for the Future Business Leaders of America**. A couple years back, our funding was cut so I couldn't take the kids on field trips or bring in speakers or anything. Another thing is that, even though we do have a school band, we don't have, um, anything in addition to it. **It would be wonderful to have a separate orchestra, uh, pep band, and maybe even, like, a jazz band or something**, but Saint Michael doesn't have the money to have all those different groups. The only sports we're able to fund are basketball, volleyball, and track. Kids that want to participate in stuff like wrestling or gymnastics can't, or I guess they join things outside school. **With the school consolidation, students from Saint Michael would have the opportunity to join a bunch of different activities that they, uh, they would never see here**. I think that would be awesome. But uh, like I said before, I've got some major concerns about the plan too. **So I'm just in a dilemma trying to decide if I like the idea or not.** I: I don't think you're the only one in that dilemma. Anything else you want to add? T: I think I covered all my main points…and my class will be getting back from lunch shortly so I probably should be getting back. I: Ok. Thanks again for taking time to visit with me.	-Benefit: Extracurriculars -Benefit: Extracurriculars -Benefit: Extracurriculars -Impact: Uncertain

3

Date of Interview: 5 November 2010
Time of Interview: 11:00 A.M.
Location of Interview: Saint Michael School
Participant Name: Donna White
Participant Position/Occupation: Retired Caterer

Interviewer: So, to get started today, could you tell me about your connection with Saint Michael School and with the Parish?	
Parishioner: I been a **member of this church for, well, since my fourth child was born, so that's what, 30 years now.** Each of my 6 kids been to the school for at least a few grades, and 4 of them went through there for all the grades. Too bad they all moved away. Otherwise, uh, all their kids, all my grandkids, would be going there too.	-Affiliation: Parishioner, 30 years
I: Wow, you've been around this area for awhile now, huh?	
P: I sure have. Me and my husband, we been living here longer than anybody that's here now. **We've seen a lot of stuff—seen the school when it was booming, seen people come and go, seen the neighborhood, um, demographic change a lot.**	-Demographic change
I: Well, you are a great person for me to be interviewing then. Now, to get down to it, can you tell me what you all know about the proposed consolidation plan?	
P: **I'll tell ya, I don't know a whole lot. 'Bout all I know is that they think, um, they think that Saint Michael can't get enough money to keep the school running,** so they want to put it together with some other schools.	-Knowledge about proposal: Combine with other schools
I: Who is "they" that you're talking about?	
P: They? Well, I think "they" is the, the uh, whatcha call it, the school board.	
I: Ok, ok. How did you find out what you know about the consolidation?	
P: **You see, I play bridge every Thursday with a group of ladies from the parish. Millie Baker's one of them ladies, and she's got two grandkids going to the school. I guess the information was in the, uh, school newsletter and her daughter read that and told her 'bout the idea, and then she, uh, passed it onto me** 'cause she knew I'd be concerned.	-Gained knowledge: Fellow parishioner

I: Ok. And…now, how do you think this consolidation would impact that school and parish community at Saint Michael?	
P: I think it's gonna be real sad, what this consolidation would do to our community. **Right now, we got a real good community with everybody in the parish. Um…that school is a real big piece of that community. If we lose that school, we lose that big piece. It'll be like all them kids will just vanish.**	-Loss of community; parish-school connection
I: But the children will still be at Mass on Sunday and at, um, other parish functions. Why do you say they would just vanish?	
P: Ok, think about this way. Let's look at the parish community as a big family. You got all these kids, grandkids, cousins, nieces, nephews, everybody just living around in one area. You, uh, you see each other all the time and every time you are together it's a great old time. Then, one of your kids moves away, taking their whole family with them. Sure, you're still related to them and you still love them, but now they're far away. You never see them anymore, save, uh, once at Christmas and maybe Easter if you're lucky. **Now your community is all changed, and is it better off? As a mom who's kids moved away, lemme tell you that no, you ain't any better off with them gone.**	-Loss of community; parish-school connection
I: That's an interesting way to put it. So, that leads me into my next question—what is your biggest concern about this proposal?	
P: Hm, the biggest…I **guess I'm just concerned about losing the school and uh, what it means to our whole community.** Saint Michael's been around for a real long time. There's been a lot of kids that passed through those doors, and a whole lot of people's lives have been touched by the school. **We shut the school down and bus the students off to some new building, what happens to all the history of the last 130 years?** I've lived in this neighborhood for 30 years. I've seen a lot of changes come around. That school's been a rock in our community. I just, I can't even imagine it just being gone. It's an idea I don't even want to think about.	-Concern: Loss of community

-Concern: Loss of historical connection |
| I: Could you elaborate a little more for me on why losing the history is such a concern to you? | |
| P: Uh, well it's just hard for me to, for me to describe it. I just think that shutting down that building and forgetting about it and, uh, all the good work it's done would just be such a shame, such a darn shame. I guess it sorta ties back into losing the, uh, | |

community aspect of the parish. **A lot of people feel tied back into the community 'cause they went to that school however many years ago. We lose the school, we lose the history, and people lose a deep tie they once had to others.**	-Loss of community; parish-school connection -Concern: Loss of historical connection
I: I see. Ok, well that does it for the questions I have for you. Is there anything you want to add before we, uh, wrap it up? P: Oh, are we coming to the end of your questions already? All this talking about the school got me all fired up about it and I'm ready to get up on my soapbox. I know a lot of people are worried about money for the school. I've, uh, I've heard a few people say that they don't even think the school has enough cash to stay open. I think that's going overboard. The thing that I've heard more people say is that the school ain't got enough money to give the kids, um, what do they say…good opportunities in academics and um, whatcha call it, um, extracurriculars. To those people I say, so what? So what if we can't afford fancy stuff like some other schools can? **Saint Michael gives our kids a good, faith-based education. And we, uh, we also provide a strong community there for our kids. It ain't all about money.** Let's go back to how I was talking about the community as a family before. Say that your kid that moved away did it because, um, they could make more money at their new job. Now they can afford all kinds of fancy stuff, but uh, they aren't happy 'cause they miss their family and friends, their community back home. Do you think they are in a better spot now, since they have more money? If that was my kid, I would tell them to get on back home. **But that's because I'm a believer in the idea that money isn't everything. This isn't the first time this school has seen hard times. We've been through it before, and we made it out.** I think, uh, it comes down to that Saint Michael does good work and we gotta have faith that we'll be ok. I: You certainly seem to have a good amount of faith yourself. P: Well, I don't think you can get through life without it. Once, when we had first moved to the area— I: Sorry to interrupt, but if you could pause for just a minute…I have everything I need for the interview so I am going to shut off the tape recorder quickly…	-Loss of community; parish-school connection -Financial challenge

Appendix B:
Presenting Your Findings

Sharing your findings is an essential component of the full action research se-quence, and there are ample opportunities to do so at the local and national level. Below is an overview of the many places and media formats our students have chosen to share their research.

Research Brief

As noted in Chapter 6, an unshared action research project is like a stone sitting next to a pond. You must confidently "throw your stone into the water" in order to create the ripple effects that you desire—whether those effects are a challenge to the status quo, an improvement in established practice, or beginning a larger dia-logue about change. Recall, too, that the pillar of Christian community that has ani-mated your action research comes to bear again at this stage of research dissemina-tion and engagement. You bless your own personal and professional community by freely and enthusiastically sharing the insights, conclusions, and recommendations gleaned from your action research.

One particularly effective mode of presenting your action research to diverse au-diences is to craft a research brief. In contrast to your fully developed action research paper, a research brief is a highly distilled version of your topic, questions, findings, and recommendations. Much like an executive summary, a research brief is a concise, reader-friendly, and objective summation of your action research. In policy advocacy circles, a research brief is often referred to as a "one-pager," and it includes "only the most pertinent information and can be an effective way to succinctly summarize ma-jor points and guide discussions with policy makers" (Izumi et al., 2010, p. 142).

Keep in mind a few strategies when crafting your own research brief (Friese & Bogenschneider, 2009; Virginia Adult Education Research Network, 2000). First, this exercise is an opportunity to be creative, especially in selecting a catchy title, designing a visually appealing layout, using white space and headings judiciously, and perhaps inserting pertinent photos or graphics. Second, avoid the use of jargon, technical language, and/or acronyms in recounting your research; direct, active voice statements convey information with clarity and impact. Third, consider illustrating your main points with concrete examples or verbatim quotes from your study participants. Fourth, since by its very nature action research seeks to be transformative, consider closing the research brief by listing immediate next steps and suggested recommendations. Finally, by design, research briefs do not contain extensive detail on research methods, limitations, and other caveats (Stocking & Sparks, 2007), so be sure to provide contact information so that interested readers can obtain these details.

Peruse the example provided at the end of this appendix to understand the content, format, and style of a practitioner-created research brief. To review several more examples of research briefs specific to action research in Catholic schools, visit http://researchandaction.wordpress.com

Conferences

Regional and national conferences are excellent venues for sharing your research and for "professional dialogue, reflection, and brainstorming" (Mertler, 209, p. 195). The call for proposals, review processes, and presentation formats vary widely across conferences, so we recommend that you investigate specific requirements at the website of the sponsoring organization. Additionally, many of these national conferences have regional or state chapters that also sponsor annual conferences or meetings. Below is a list of conferences and conference websites for some of the more popular venues to present your Catholic school action research project. Also, see the example action research posters at the end of this appendix for ideas about how to prepare and present your findings in a conference poster.

1. **The Mary Ann Remick Leadership Conference**
   http://researchandaction.wordpress.com/

The Remick Leadership Conference is hosted annually at the University of Notre Dame highlighting the innovative action research projects of the graduates of the Mary Ann Remick Leadership Program, and other teachers and leaders in Catholic education.

2. **National Catholic Educational Association (NCEA)**
   http://www.ncea.org

NCEA's annual gathering provides Catholic school teachers and leaders an opportunity to network with colleagues in Catholic education and attend professional development and presentation sessions on a wide array of issues in Catholic education.

3. **American Educational Research Association (AERA)**
     http://www.aera.net

AERA is the largest educational research organization representing thousands of education practitioners and researchers form all parts of the world. This large organization is comprised of divisions and special interest groups (SIGs) that represent focused research interests such as Catholic Education and Action Research.

Action Research on the Internet

Blogging about your action research project—the journey and the results—can be a natural extension of the intentional focus on community that inspired your inquiry in the first place. Individual action researchers, local groups of teachers, and faculty in departments or colleges of education sponsor a variety of websites and blogs that may be of interest as you explore the many derivations of action research, and seek opportunities to share your work with others. Below is an abbreviated list of some action research blogs and websites:

1. **Catholic Action Research Network**
     http://researchandaction.wordpress.com/

The Catholic Action Research Network blog is maintained by the authors of this text as a site to share insights and suggestions for successfully navigating your AR project, a repository of downloadable conference posters from the annual Remick Leadership Conference, and an on-line community for dialogue about action research in Catholic education.

2. **Center for Collaborative Action Research**
     http://cadres.pepperdine.edu/ccar/

The Center for Collaborative Action Research is hosted by the graduate school of education and psychology at Pepperdine University and features graduate level action research projects, opportunities to present your action research, and additional electronic and print resources for conducting action research in education- and community-based settings.

3. **The Collaborative Action Research Network**
     http://www.did.stu.mmu.ac.uk/carnnew/index.php

The Collaborative Action Research Network is an international organization sponsored and maintained by faculty at universities from throughout the United Kingdom.

The website provides valuable resources for novice and experienced action researchers, and features an archive of the proceedings from their annual international action research conference.

Academic Journals

Publishing your action research in an academic journal provides an opportunity for broad circulation of your work and "helps bridge the divide between research and application" (Mertler, 2009, p. 193). The submission requirements vary by journal, but typically include a cover letter addressed to the editor, a blinded manuscript for peer review, and possibly a checklist or other documentation ensuring that all publication requirements have been met. The journals included in the list below focus on action research and Catholic education broadly; you may also wish to seek out other academic journals dedicated to the specific topic of your action research inquiry (e.g., teacher evaluation, literacy, after school programs, etc.).

1. *Catholic Education: A Journal of Inquiry and Practice*
http://ejournals.bc.edu/ojs/index.php/catholic

Catholic Education is "a refereed, open access, online journal that promotes and disseminates scholarship about the purposes, practices, and issues in Catholic education at all levels" (*Catholic Education*, 2011).

2. *Action Research Journal*
http://arj.sagepub.com/

Action Research is "a new international, interdisciplinary, peer reviewed, quarterly published refereed journal which is a forum for the development of the theory and practice of action research" (*Action Research*, 2011).

3. *Educational Action Research*
http://www.tandf.co.uk/journals/titles/09650792.asp

Educational Action Research is a "fully refereed international journal concerned with exploring the dialogue between research and practice in educational settings" (*Educational Action Research*, 2011).

4. *i.e.: inquiry in education*
    http://digitalcommons.nl.edu/ie/

Peer-reviewed and published online by the Center for Practitioner Research at National Louis University, the "journal serves as a forum for scholarly work pertaining to practitioner research. The journal features original practitioner research studies, theoretical articles pertaining to practitioner research, descriptions of practitioner research centers and book reviews" (*i.e.: inquiry in education*, 2011).

AR Insight

" Once you have completed your project, it is very rewarding knowing your action research really does make a difference at your school. I saw positive results after only one semester. Action research is also a great way to build community at your school. I found the people involved in my research felt a sense of ownership by participating in the project and were interested in knowing the results of my surveys. "

Our students have found that sharing their action research along the way—getting feedback on small sections of the paper—is also quite useful. One student encouraged his classmates to "share your hard work with your colleagues at school....A second or third pair of eyes might notice errors in research or design, while also providing insight."

Sample Conference Posters and Research Briefs

The following pages contain exemplary conference posters and research briefs created by graduates of the Mary Ann Remick Leadership Program in the Alliance for Catholic Education. These products of the action research sequence concisely present core elements of the action research project in an engaging, appealing, and easy-to-read format. We hope these select examples will inspire you to think creatively about how to best share your own action research project with valued stakeholders in your community and beyond.

Analysis of Special Education at Christ the King School

Johnnathan Combs

University of Notre Dame and Christ the King Catholic School

BACKGROUND

The Archdiocese of Indianapolis has made a concerted effort to reach students with special needs. Over the past fifteen years, all of the north deanery schools have successfully implemented special needs programs. Christ the King (CKS) grade school is one of the north deanery schools located in Indianapolis, IN

➢ Recognized as a Blue Ribbon School of Excellence

➢ Enrollment is 397

➢ In the past five years the special need department has grown from 40 to more than 74 students with no additional faculty or staff.

CURRENT STUDY

While public schools have a legal obligation to serve students with special needs, CKS recognizes that Catholic schools have a moral obligation to educate all children of God and is committed to seeking out and providing best practices that will allow inclusion of all students.

Purpose Statement

The purpose of this action research project was to explore the perceptions and attitudes of principal and teachers towards the inclusion of students with special needs at Christ the King School and develop policies and procedures for best practices.

Research Questions

➢ What are the perceptions and attitudes of the school principal and teachers toward the inclusion of students with special needs at Christ the King School?

➢ What are best practices in special education classes in Archdiocese of Indianapolis north deanery schools?

METHOD

Mixed Method Design

An original survey instrument was deployed to all faculty at CKS (n=25) on surveymonkey.com with a 96% return rate

Qualitative semi-structured interviews (n=2) of professionals holding a PhD in Special Education

FINDINGS

Quantitative

The majority (67%) of respondents at CKS either agreed or strongly agreed that they have adequate *resources* to teach students with disabilities and 100% believe that students with special needs have a right to a Catholic education.

When asked if DIBELS assessments help identify at risk students in reading, a high percentage (79%) of the faculty responded positively. Additionally, 71% utilize DIBELS to plan reading lessons.

Qualitative

The interviewees agreed on many best practices including the following:

➢ Avoid "cookie cutter" programs

➢ Continuously evaluate the children

➢ Response to Intervention (RTI), is a best practice

➢ Use technology (not necessarily high tech) to engage the students

The interviewees disagreed about the effectiveness of push in/pull out programs.

Summary

The results of the survey were mostly as expected, with the faculty ready, willing and able to work with students with special needs even with the lack of resources available at CKS versus public schools. In addition, based upon the interviews, CKS is in line with the best practices when working with students with special needs.

DISCUSSION AND EXTENSION

➢ While a majority (54%) of respondents were positive about being adequately *trained* for teaching students with disabilities in their classroom, a high percentage (46%) responded negatively, which may show the need to increase training to the faculty.

➢ While there is some concern about inadequate training when it comes to working with students with special needs, the programs already in place are assisting all staff members.

➢ Through analysis and extrapolating the findings, the next steps will consist of the annual evaluation of programs and policies to ensure proper evaluation and implementation of inclusion at CKS.

➢ CKS will implement internal workshops to train staff with latest procedures in addition to refreshing current policies and procedures

Poster presented at the 3rd Annual ACE Leadership Conference.
Address correspondence to

Jon Combs   5858 N. Crittenden Avenue Indianapolis IN 46220   jcombs@cks-indy.org

All Are Welcome

Analysis of Special Education at Christ the King School, Indianapolis, IN

Snapshot

- Recognized as a Blue Ribbon School of Excellence
- Enrollment is 397
- In the past five years the special need department has grown from 40 to more than 74 students with no additional faculty or staff.

Method

- A quantitative original survey instrument deployed to all faculty at CKS (n=25) on surveymonkey.com with a 96% return rate
- Qualitative semi-structured interviews (n=2) of professionals holding a PhD in Special Education

Survey Summary

The results of the survey were mostly as expected, with the faculty ready, willing and able to work with students with special needs even with the lack of resources available at CKS versus public schools. In addition, based upon the interviews, CKS is in line with the best practices when working with students with special needs.

Current Study

Christ the King (CKS) grade school is one of the north deanery schools located in Indianapolis, IN. The Archdiocese of Indianapolis has made a concerted effort to reach students with special needs.

The purpose of this action research project was to explore the perceptions and attitudes of principal and teachers towards the inclusion of students with special needs at Christ the King School and develop policies and procedures for best practices.

Research Questions

1) What are the perceptions and attitudes of the school principal and teachers toward the inclusion of students with special needs at Christ the King School?

2) What are best practices in special education classes in Archdiocese of Indianapolis north deanery schools?

Findings and Discussion

The majority (67%) of respondents at CKS either agreed or strongly agreed that they have adequate *resources* to teach students with disabilities and 100% believe that students with special needs have a right to a Catholic education.

When asked if DIBELS assessments help identify at risk students in reading, a high percentage (79%) of the faculty responded positively. Additionally, 71% utilize DIBELS to plan reading lessons.

While a majority (54%) of respondents were positive about being adequately *trained* for teaching students with disabilities in their classroom, a high percentage (46%) responded negatively, which may show the need to increase training to the faculty.

Through analysis and extrapolating the findings, the next steps will consist of the annual evaluation of programs and policies to ensure proper evaluation and implementation of inclusion at CKS.

CKS will implement internal workshops to train staff with latest procedures in addition to refreshing current policies and procedures

While there is some concern about inadequate training when it comes to working with students with special needs, the programs already in place are assisting all staff members.

Johnnathan Combs • 5858 N. Crittenden Avenue, Indianapolis IN 46220 • jcombs@cks-indy.org

Benilde-St. Margaret's

Servant-Leadership Infusion

Zachary Zeckser
Benilde-St. Margaret's School
University of Notre Dame

BACKGROUND

BSM created a co-curricular student group, the Student Leadership Forum (SLF), to infuse the student body with servant-leadership. With no research addressing servant-leadership in high schools, this project's vision relied primarily on Church documents and Greenleaf's model.

• *The Religious Dimension of Education in a Catholic School* stated that, "[we]… must take into account … the call of each one to be an active and creative agent in service to society" (1988, para. 63).

• Greenleaf says that servant-leadership "begins with the natural feeling that one wants to serve, to serve first. Then, … to aspire to lead" (Greenleaf Center for Servant Leadership, 2009, para. 1).

CURRENT STUDY

The document *Lay Catholics in Schools* said that "these [servant] attitudes must be encouraged in the students" (Sacred Congregation for Catholic Education, 1982, para. 30). Following this direction, the SLF was taught servant-leadership and was provided opportunities to practice it and lead the school in its practice.

Purpose Statement

The purpose of this action research was to assess the impact of the SLF on the degree to which students view their peers as servant-leaders and to determine what actions of the SLF most impacted these views.

Research Questions

Do BSM students view their peers as servant-leaders? What servant-leader traits to students possess or lack? How did the SLF impact student behaviors and attitudes? What aspects of the SLF did its members identify as most and least helpful in promoting servant-leadership?

METHOD

Participants completing the surveys included 30 students from each grade. They were performed in September and February. The SLF excluded grades 7-8, so t-tests with higher gains in grades 9-12 would show the SLF was effective. Interviews included only SLF students and were held following the data survey analysis. Interviews were transcribed, coded, and collapsed for themes.

FINDINGS

The pretest indicated that BSM students already viewed their peers as servant-leaders, so improving their scores was not uniformly achieved. While the quantitative data lacked the statistic significance to demonstrate the SLF effective, the qualitative data did offer four major factors for its success.

These factors arose when the participants were asked very broad questions ascertaining the best and worst aspects of the SLF and for possible ways to help it better achieve its goals. The four major themes include a major project, group collaboration, facilitator media, and increased meetings.

The qualitative data indicated that the members of the SLF viewed it very positively. They unanimously agreed that it helped them develop their servant-leadership traits. The three most common themes showed approval for SLF. The fourth most common concept offered, though, was a suggestion for how to modify the group to help it improve.

Major Collapsed Codes with Representative Quotations from Focus Group Interviews

Code	Number of references	Representative quotation
Interest in a unique capstone project	48	"a really neat way to promote service and … leadership".
Appreciation of group collaboration	33	"Everyone just became really more involved".
Appreciation for media sent by facilitator	21	"examples of it actually being put into action".
Desire for more frequent meetings	17	"you need that communication". "constant … update".

DISCUSSION AND EXTENSION

While the lack research time constraints limited the capacity for the SLF to make a statistically significant impact on student perceptions of their peers, SLF did provide the basis for a unique and impactful servant-leadership program.

• The facilitator of the SLF began to implement changes. Because of the students' appreciation for the media they had received, the members began to receive media via email with increased frequency to enhance their servant-leadership.

• The SLF coordinated a second project, enlisting the youth and adults to volunteer for three consecutive evenings packing meals for infants in developing countries. Over 150 volunteers packaged 77,000 meals and offered uniformly positive feedback, insisting that we repeat twice next year.

• The facilitator created a schedule for next year that nearly doubles the number of meetings. At half of the meetings, the returning members of the SLF, who are receiving additional servant-leadership training, will teach new members.

• The SLF facilitator asked club advisors to invite students with servant traits to participate in the SLF next year.

• A fall pretest will be sent to another sample of staff, and students with a spring posttest. If t-tests show significant increased gains in grades 9-12 over grades 7-8, BSM will know it has a program worth introducing to other schools.

Poster presented at the 3rd Annual ACE Leadership Conference.
Address correspondence to Zachary Zeckser, 6711 Girard Avenue South, Richfield, MN, 55423 zzeckser@nd.edu

Research Brief January 2011

Servant-leadership

The Student Leadership Forum at Benilde – St. Margaret's School

"Becoming a servant-leader begins with the natural feeling that one wants to serve, to serve first. Then conscious choice brings one to aspire to lead."
-Robert K. Greenleaf

A new model for high schools

What we did

Combine We created a student forum combining a few students from six clubs.

Communicate Students shared the opportunities available through their clubs.

Collaborate Students shared the other clubs' events with their own club members.

Cultivate The forum advisor coached the students in servant-leadership.

Create The forum created opportunities to embody servant-leadership.

Findings

What worked:

- Capstone events

- Club collaboration

- Engaging media

Other take-aways:

- Students asked for more meetings

- Returning members will coach newcomers

"It helped me understand that you really do need to serve people in order to be a leader."
–Dan, Student Leadership Forum Member

Contact Zachary Zeckser at zzeckser@bsm-online.org

Response to Student Literacy Needs

Jennifer Beltramo
University of Notre Dame - Mother of Sorrows School

BACKGROUND

The present condition of literacy in the United States is alarming. Nearly 90% of intermediate and middle school students from low-income families are not proficient in reading. Mother of Sorrows School in South-Central Los Angeles has not been immune to this problem.

- 232 students (PK-8)
- 93% Latino, 7% African American
- 98% qualify for free lunch
- 77% English language learners
- 63% (4th-8th) read below grade level
- 85% (7th) perform below proficiency, 48% of whom have deficits of 3 or 4 years

CURRENT STUDY

Research identifies a pressing need for the implementation of multi-component reading interventions. These interventions should be intensive and sustained. They should incorporate both lower and higher-order skills as well as opportunities for independent application to narrative and expository texts.

Purpose Statement
The purpose of this action research project was to determine the effectiveness of a reading intervention program on improving mastery of fluency, word study, and comprehension for students in Grades 4-8.

Research Questions
•Does the reading intervention program improve student performance on standardized fluency, word study, and comprehension assessments?
•Does the reading intervention program influence student perceptions of reading?

METHOD

This quantitative study was conducted from August 2010 through March 2011 using a quasi-experimental within group design with 112 students from Grades 4-8.

Four instruments were used: *MASI-R* oral reading fluency measures, *Words Their Way* spelling inventories, *Gates-MacGinitie Reading Test*, and an original survey instrument with a 4-point Likert scale.

Multiple, tiered interventions were implemented based on each student's performance on the initial assessments.

FINDINGS

The data indicated the overall effectiveness of the multi-component reading intervention program.

Separate t-tests revealed that all five grades achieved a statistically significant increase between pretest and posttest scores for all three areas of reading: fluency, word study, and comprehension.

All grades made above average gains in reading comprehension and ended the study on or above grade level. Students in Grade 7 made the largest average gains ($M = 1.78$, $SD = 1.82$). Students in Grades 5 and 6 also averaged more than 1.5 years growth.

The number of students in Grades 4-8 performing on or above grade level increased from 37% on the pretest to 61% on the posttest. Grade 6 had the largest increase (43% to 87%).

An ANOVA revealed that students were able to make comparable gains regardless of their initial performance above or below grade level.

Student perceptions of reading confidence were positive for all grades, while perceptions of independent strategy use varied for each grade.

FINDINGS

Mean and Standard Deviation for Comprehension Gain Score Relative to Initial Grade Equivalent Ranges

Pretest Grade Equivalent	Comprehension Gain Score	
	M	SD
2.1+ above	1.88	0.78
1.1-2.0 above	1.61	1.29
0.1-1.0 above	1.86	2.23
On level	1.40	2.25
0.1-1.0 below	1.37	1.39
1.1-2.0 below	1.38	1.41
2.1+ below	1.33	1.00

Note. Average growth during the same time period would reflect a comprehension gain score of 0.68

DISCUSSION AND EXTENSION

The research-based reading intervention program was effective not only for the students 2+ years above level but also for those 2+ years below level, 38% of whom had been diagnosed with learning disabilities.

As a result, this program will be continued and extended to the entire school community.

The findings were shared with local Catholic school principals and components of the program will be incorporated into their curriculum during the 2011-2012 school year.

Looking forward, the administration and faculty at Mother of Sorrows School will begin a new action research project to study the extent to which comprehension strategy rubrics can foster student self-awareness of independent strategy use.

Poster presented at the 4th Annual Remick Leadership Conference. Address correspondence to Jennifer Beltramo, 100 W 87th Pl, Los Angeles, CA, 90003, jennifer.beltramo@la-archdiocese.org

Beating the Odds

A Response to Urban Student Literacy Needs

Pressing Issue

The present condition of literacy in the United States is alarming. Nearly 90% of intermediate and middle school students from low-income families are not proficient in reading. Mother of Sorrows School in South-Central Los Angeles has not been immune to this problem.

- 232 students (PK-8)
- 93% Latino, 7% African American
- 98% qualify for free lunch
- 77% English language learners
- 63% (4th-8th) read below grade level
- 85% (7th) perform below proficiency, 48% of whom have deficits of 3 or 4 years

Current Study

Research identifies a pressing need for the implementation of multi-component reading interventions. These interventions should be intensive and sustained. They should incorporate both lower and higher-order skills as well as opportunities for independent application to narrative and expository texts.

The purpose of this action research project was to determine the effectiveness of a reading intervention program on improving mastery of fluency, word study, and comprehension for students in grades four through eight.

"It will never be possible to free the needy from their poverty unless they are first freed from the impoverishment arising from the lack of adequate education."

John Paul II, 1999, no. 71

Method

The study was conducted from August 2010 through June 2011 using a quasi-experimental within group design with 112 students from grades 4-8.

Area of Reading	Instrument	Tiered Interventions
Fluency	MASI-R oral reading fluency measures	Great Leaps program Choral reads Sound/spelling, high frequency word, and passage practice
Word Study	Words Their Way spelling inventories	Words Their Way
Comprehension	Gates-MacGinitie Reading Tests	SRA Reading Laboratory Accelerated Reader Instruction in and application of 7 reading comprehension strategies

Mother of Sorrows School • 100 West 87th Place • Los Angeles, CA 90003 • 323-758-6204

Mother of Sorrows School is guided by the Vincentian charism to honor Christ "as the source and model of all charity, serving Him corporally and spiritually in the person of the poor" (Congregation of the Mission, 2004, p. 28).

The number of students in grades 4-8 performing on or above grade level increased from 37% on the pretest to 83% on the posttest.

Findings

Separate *t*-tests revealed that all five grades achieved a statistically significant increase between pretest and posttest scores for all three areas of reading: fluency, word study, and comprehension.

All grades made above average gains in reading comprehension and ended the study above grade level. Students in grade 7 made the largest average gains (M = 3.09, SD = 1.77).

The number of students in grades 4-8 performing on or above grade level increased from 37% on the pretest to 83% on the posttest.

Comprehension Gain Score Relative to Initial Grade Equivalent Ranges	
Pretest Grade Equivalent	Gain Score
2+ above	2.23
1.1-2.0 above	3.21
0.1-1.0 above	3.10
On level	2.45
0.1-1.0 below	2.47
1.1-2.0 below	2.64
2+ below	2.36

Note. Average growth during the same time period would reflect a comprehension gain score of 1.00

An ANOVA revealed that students were able to make comparable gains regardless of their initial performance above or below grade level.

Reading Comprehension Grade Equivalents		
Class	Pretest Scores	Posttest Scores
Grade 4	4.03	6.37
Grade 5	4.70	7.65
Grade 6	5.68	7.78
Grade 7	5.77	8.75
Grade 8	7.96	9.88

Discussion and Extension

Faculty collaboration during the study led to the development of an innovative program for reading instruction based on multiple, scaffolded exposures of reading comprehension strategies applied to diverse texts.

In response to the Church's social teachings, Catholic schools have a moral imperative to implement programs that will support the needs of all children. The urgency of meeting those needs becomes even greater when our schools serve those who are marginalized by society. At a time when the lack of adequate education is glaringly apparent across the nation, the tremendous dedication of Catholic educators is yielding exceptional results. If this commitment to research-based practices is sustained, "historians will look back on our age and marvel that against great odds, we changed the ending" (Notre Dame Task Force, 2006, p. 19).

For more information, please contact Jennifer Beltramo at jennifer.beltramo@la-archdiocese.org

About the Authors

Anthony C. Holter is Faculty in The Mary Ann Remick Leadership Program in the Alliance for Catholic Education and Concurrent Assistant Professor of Psychology at the University of Notre Dame. Holter recently co-authored *Research, Action, and Change: Leaders Reshaping Catholic Schools* with colleagues in the Remick Leadership Program. These tandem texts highlight his interest in examining how sound educational research methods support and animate core tenets of the Catholic faith tradition. Holter also conducts research on effective measures of Catholic identity for Catholic schools. He holds a B.A. in Theology and Humanities from Saint Mary's University of Minnesota, a Master's degree in Education from the University of Notre Dame, and a Master's degree and Ph.D. in Educational Psychology from the University of Wisconsin —Madison.

James M. Frabutt is Faculty in The Mary Ann Remick Leadership Program in the Alliance for Catholic Education and Concurrent Associate Professor of Psychology at the University of Notre Dame. With colleagues in the Remick Leadership Program, he has co-authored two books, *Research, Action, and Change: Leaders Reshaping Catholic Schools*, and *Faith, Finances, and the Future: The Notre Dame Study of U.S. Pastors*. He has employed action-oriented, community-based research approaches to areas such as juvenile delinquency prevention, school-based mental health, teacher/administrator inquiry, racial disparities in the juvenile justice system, and community violence reduction. He holds a B.A. in Psychology and Italian from the University of Notre Dame and a Master's degree and Ph.D. in Human Development and Family Studies from the University of North Carolina at Greensboro.

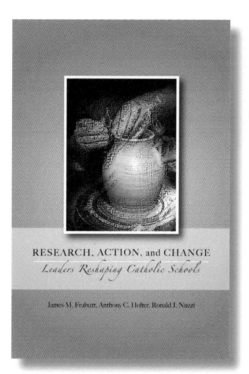